THE
ECONOMY
of God

WITNESS LEE

Living Stream Ministry
Anaheim, California • www.lsm.org

First Edition, 1968.

ISBN 0-87083-415-0

Published by

Living Stream Ministry

2431 W. La Palma Ave., Anaheim, CA 92801 U.S.A.

P. O. Box 2121, Anaheim, CA 92814 U.S.A.

Printed in the United States of America

04   05   06   07   08   09   /   15   14   13   12   11

CONTENTS

FOREWORD

The following chapters are the messages given in the Summer Conference of 1964 at Los Angeles. The spoken form has been retained. The author would urge all the readers to give their attention to the spiritual reality conveyed in these messages rather than to the language itself.

The word "economy" used in the title of this volume may sound somewhat strange to the reader. "The economy of God" is a quotation from 1 Timothy 1:4, according to the Greek. "Economy" is the Greek word "oikonomia" which primarily signifies the household management, the household administration, arrangement and distribution, or dispensation (of wealth, property, affairs, etc.). It is used with the intention of stressing the focal point of God's divine enterprise, which is to distribute, or dispense, Himself into man.

The three Persons in the Godhead are for God's economy, the divine distribution, the holy dispensation. The Father as the source is embodied in the Son, and the Son as the course is realized in the Spirit as the transmission. God the Father is a Spirit (John 4:24), and God the Son, as the last Adam, was made a life-giving Spirit (1 Cor. 15:45). All is in God the Spirit, which is the Holy Spirit revealed in the New Testament. This Holy Spirit today, with the fullness of the Father in the riches of the Son, has come into our human spirit and dwells there to impart all that God is into our very being. This is God's economy, the divine dispensation. The Holy Spirit of God, dwelling in our human spirit to dispense all that God is in Christ into our being, is the focus, the very mark of this mysterious distribution of the Triune God. This is the battleground of the spiritual warfare. Oh, how much the subtle enemy has been and still is distracting the saints of God, even the seeking ones, from this mark of God's economy by so many good and even scriptural things. In such a time of confusion, as in the time when the Epistles to Timothy were written, we must be narrowed down and even zeroed in to the all-inclusive divine Spirit in our human spirit that we may be kept from missing the mark of the divine economy. Therefore, the returning to, the abiding in, and the exercising of our spirit to realize the Spirit of God is basically necessary today. It is by so doing that we may partake of all the fullness of God by enjoying the unsearchable riches of Christ. May the Lord grant us grace that we may be brought into such a realization and that we may practice it in our daily life and in all that we do.

For a proper application and better result, all the messages in this book need to be read with a praying spirit. It will be more profitable to pray-read all the quotations of the Scripture in every chapter and always accompany the reading with prayer. May the Lord's presence with His sweet anointing within be realized by all the readers in their reading of these messages in the spirit.

Witness Lee

Los Angeles, California, U.S.A.
January 11, 1968

CHAPTER ONE

THE ECONOMY OF THE TRIUNE GOD

My burden in all the messages I am giving here is to share with you something of God's economy. Let us read 1 Timothy chapter one, verses 3 through 7: "...that thou mightest charge certain men not to teach a different doctrine, neither to give heed to fables and endless genealogies, which minister questionings, rather than a dispensation of God (Gk. *God's economy*) which is in faith; so do I now. But the end of the charge is love out of a pure heart and a good conscience and faith unfeigned: from which things some having swerved (Gk. *missed the mark*) have turned aside unto vain talking; desiring to be teachers of the law...."*

These verses contain two very important phrases as indicated in Greek, the original language of the New Testament: "God's economy" and "missed the mark." The Apostle Paul was chosen by God to bear the responsibility for God's economy, and he trained his spiritual son, Timothy, in this economy. It is quite interesting to note that Paul's epistle to Timothy was written at a time when many Christians had drifted from the original pathway. They had missed the central mark of God's economy and were paying attention to something else.

THE DISTRACTIONS FROM GOD'S ECONOMY

According to history two prevailing elements distracted the early Christians from the right track: Judaism and Gnosticism. Both the Judaizers with their religious doctrines and

* Scripture quotations are from the American
Standard Version unless otherwise indicated.

forms and the Gnostics with their philosophies deterred the Christians from following the Lord in the pathway of God's economy. Apparently, it was the good elements of Judaism and Gnosticism that sidetracked these early Christians. If these elements were not comparatively good, they could never have been prevailing enough to cause the believers to miss the mark of God's economy. For instance, the Judaizers strongly stressed the Mosaic Law of the Old Testament. There certainly was nothing wrong with the Law. On the contrary, it was unquestionably right and good and was given directly by God Himself. But the Law of itself was not related to the mark of God's economy. Gnosticism, from the human point of view, also had its good principles. In fact, it was one of the best inventions of human civilization and was a kind of help to the heathen. But the Gnostics tried to bring their philosophy into the church, distracting the early Christians from the mark of God's economy.

Today, even though there are no Judaizers or Gnostics to disturb us, there is still much to distract us. For nearly twenty centuries the subtle one has never ceased using the seemingly good things to divert believers from following the Lord in the right track. If we spend time with the Lord, we will realize that the enemy is persistent in utilizing even the good things of Christianity to distract the Lord's children from the mark of God's economy. While I was traveling through many districts in this country during the last few years, I realized that many religious matters and even scriptural things have been used by the subtle enemy to influence seeking Christians to depart from the pathway of God's economy.

THE DEFINITION OF GOD'S ECONOMY

What is God's economy? The Scriptures, composed of sixty-six books, contain many different teachings, but if we would make a thorough and careful study of the Scriptures with spiritual insight, we would realize that God's economy is simply His plan to *dispense Himself into humanity*. God's economy is God's dispensation, which means nothing else than God dispensing Himself into the human race. It is regrettable that the term "dispensation" has been misused by Christianity. Its definition is nearly the same as the Greek word "economy." It means the administrative arrangement, the governmental management, or the dispensing, distributing stewardship of God's plan. In this divine dispensation God, who is almighty and all-inclusive, intends to dispense nothing other than *Himself* to us. This needs to be repeated many times in order to impress us deeply!

God is exceedingly rich. He is like a successful businessman who has an enormous amount of capital. God has a business in this universe, and His vast wealth is His capital. We do not realize how many billions, countless billions, He has. All of this capital is simply *Himself,* and with it He intends to "manufacture" *Himself* in mass production. God *Himself* is the Businessman, the Capital, and the Product. His intention is to dispense Himself to many people in mass production and free of charge. Therefore, God requires such a divine arrangement, a divine management, a divine dispensation, a divine economy in order to bring Himself into humanity.

Let's be more specific. Now that we know God's purpose is to dispense Himself, we must discover *what* God is in order to know *what* He is dispensing. In other words, what is the substance of God? When a businessman plans to manufacture a product, he must, first of all, be clear about the substance, or its basic constituent. God's substance is Spirit (John 4:24). The very essence of the almighty, all-inclusive, universal God is simply Spirit. God is the Manufacturer, and He intends to reproduce Himself as the Product; therefore, whatever He reproduces must be Spirit, the very substance of Himself.

THE STEPS OF GOD'S ECONOMY

We have seen God's purpose and what is dispensed by God; now we must realize *how* God is dispensed through His economy. In other words, Spirit is what God dispenses into man, but now we need to see the means by which He does this. It is by the Trinity. The Triune God—the Father, the Son, and the Holy Spirit—is the very economy of the Godhead. Christianity during the past centuries has had many teachings about the

Trinity, but the Trinity can never be adequately understood unless it is related to the divine economy. Why are all three Persons of the Godhead required for the development of His economy? We know that the Father, the Son, and the Holy Spirit are not three different Gods, but one God, who is expressed in three Persons. Yet, what is the purpose of there being three Persons of the Godhead? Why is there God the Father, God the Son, and also God the Holy Spirit? It is because only through the Trinity can the essential means be provided whereby His Spirit is dispensed into us.

Second Corinthians 13:14 shows the steps of God's economy by the Trinity. "The grace of the Lord Jesus Christ, and the love of God, and the communion of the Holy Spirit be with you all." Here we have the grace of the Son, the love of the Father, and the communion of the Holy Spirit. What are these? Are these three different Gods? Are love, grace, and communion three different items? No. Love, grace, and communion are one element in three stages: love is the source, grace is the expression of love, and communion is the transmission of this love in grace. Likewise, God, Christ, and the Holy Spirit are one God expressed in three Persons: God is the source, Christ is the expression of God, and the Holy Spirit is the transmission bringing God in Christ into man. Thus, the three Persons of the Trinity become the three successive steps in the process of God's economy. Without these three stages, God's essence could never be dispensed into man. The economy of God is developed *from* the Father, *in* the Son, and *through* the Spirit.

(1) FROM THE FATHER

God the Father is the universal source of all things. He is invisible and unapproachable. How can God the Father, who dwells in unapproachable light (1 Tim. 6:16), be within us? How can we see the invisible Father? If God is only a Father, He would be inaccessible and could not be dispensed into man. But through the divine arrangement of His economy, He put Himself into His Son, the second Person of the Trinity, in order to make Himself available to man. All the fullness of the Father dwells in the Son (Col. 1:19; 2:9) and is expressed through the Son (John 1:18). The Father, as the inexhaustible source of everything, is embodied in the Son. The incomprehensible God is now expressed in Christ, the Word of God (John 1:1); the invisible God is revealed in Christ, the Image of God (Col. 1:15). So, the Son and the Father are one (John 10:30), and the Son is even called the Father (Isa. 9:6).

Formerly it was impossible for man to contact the Father. He was exclusively God and His nature was exclusively divine. There was nothing in the Father to bridge the gap between God and man. But now He has not only embodied Himself within the Son, He has also become incarnate in human nature. The Father was pleased to combine His own divinity with humanity in the Son. Through the incarnation of the Son, the unapproachable Father is now approachable to man. By this, man can *see* the Father, *touch* the Father, and *commune* with the Father through the Son.

We can demonstrate this relationship by dipping a white handkerchief into blue dye. The Father's divinity could originally be likened to the white handkerchief. This handkerchief, dipped into blue dye, represents the Father in the Son becoming incarnate in humanity. The white article has now become blue. Just as blue was added to the handkerchief, so the human nature was added to the divine nature, and the once separated natures have become one. The first stage of God dispensing Himself into man, therefore, is through the embodiment and incarnation of Himself in the Son as a man— thus, reproducing Himself in man.

(2) IN THE SON

The second step of bringing God into man is through the second Person of the Trinity, the Son of God. In order to understand the second stage of the economy of God, we need to know what Christ is. What are the elements that make up Christ? What are the ingredients combined together that constitute Christ?

There are seven basic elements that make up this wonderful Person, six of which were added through His history. First, Christ is the divine embodiment of God. This first element in Christ is God's divine essence and nature.

The second element, His incarnation, is the mingling of His divine nature with the human nature. Through His incarnation He brought God into man and mingled the divine essence of God with humanity. In Christ there is not only God, but also man.

The third element which was added to His divine and human natures was His human living. This glorious God-man lived on earth for thirty-three and a half years and experienced all the common and ordinary things that make up the daily human life. The Gospel of John, which emphasizes that He is the Son of God, also tells us that He was tired, hungry, thirsty, and that He wept. His human sufferings were also part of His daily life, which included many earthly troubles, problems, trials and persecutions.

His experience of death is the fourth element. He went down into death. But He not only *stepped into* death, He *passed through* death. This produced a very effective death. The death of Adam is terrible and chaotic, but the death of Christ is wonderful and effective. The death of Adam *enslaved* us to death, whereas the death of Christ *released* us from death. Although the fall of Adam brought many evil elements into us, the effective death of Christ is the killing power within us to slay all the elements of Adam's nature.

Therefore, in Christ there is the divine nature, the human nature, the daily human life with its sufferings and also the effectiveness of His death. But there are three additional elements in Christ. The fifth element is His resurrection. After His resurrection, Christ did not put off His manhood to become solely God again. Christ is still a man! And as man He has the additional element of resurrection life mingled with His humanity.

The sixth element in Christ is His ascension. By His ascension to the heavens, He transcended over all enemies, principalities, powers, dominions and authorities. All are under His feet. Mingled with Him, therefore, is the transcendent power of His ascension.

Finally, the seventh element in Christ is His enthronement. Christ, the man with the divine nature, is enthroned in the third heaven as the exalted Head of the whole universe.

He is in the heavenlies as the Lord of lords and the King of kings.

We need to remember, then, the seven wonderful elements that are in Him: the divine nature, the human nature, the daily human life with its earthly sufferings, the effectiveness of His death, the resurrection power, the transcendent power of His ascension, and the enthronement. All these elements are mingled in this one marvelous Christ.

(3) THROUGH THE SPIRIT

God, however, cannot come into us through the Son. According to the first stages of His economy, the Father placed Himself in the Son, and the Son has the seven elements mingled within Himself. But we still need another stage, a third and final step, for God to dispense Himself into man. The first step was that the Father embodied Himself in the Son; the second step was that the Son became incarnate in humanity to have all the seven wonderful elements mingled within Him; the third step is that both the Father and the Son are now in the Spirit. All that is in the Father is in the Son, and both the Father and the Son, containing all the elements in Christ, are brought into the Spirit.

The Holy Spirit, after the Lord's ascension, is no longer the same as the Spirit of God in the Old Testament times. The Spirit of God in the Old Testament had only one element—the divine nature of God. As the divine Spirit, He did not have the elements of the human nature, the daily human life, the effectiveness of death, the resurrection, the ascension and the enthronement. Today, however, under the New Testament economy all the seven elements of Christ have been placed in the Spirit, and as such this all-inclusive Spirit has come *into* us and *upon* us. In other words, He is in us and we are in Him. This is the real mingling of God with man, which we may experience at any time. We are mingled inwardly and outwardly with the Holy Spirit.

What is the Holy Spirit? He is the Spirit of Truth (John 15:26). But what is truth? The meaning of the Greek word "truth" is reality. Therefore, the Holy Spirit is the Spirit of Reality, the full reality of Christ. Just as God is embodied in

Christ, so Christ is realized in the wonderful Person of the Holy Spirit. Christ is not separate from God, and the Spirit is not separate from Christ. Christ is God expressed, and the Spirit is Christ realized in reality.

"Now the Lord is the Spirit" (2 Cor. 3:17). This verse proves that the Holy Spirit is not separate from Christ. The Lord is Christ Himself and is referred to as the Spirit. "The last Adam became a life-giving spirit" (1 Cor. 15:45). Again, the Scriptures point out that Christ, the last Adam, is the Spirit. We must admit that this life-giving Spirit is the Holy Spirit.

Furthermore, God the Father is also the Spirit (John 4:24). Hence, all three Persons of the Godhead are the Spirit. If God the Father is not the Spirit, how could He be in us, and how could we contact Him? Moreover, if God the Son is not the Spirit, how could He be in us, and how could we experience Him? Because the Father and the Son are both the Spirit, we may easily contact God and experience Christ.

Notice the following verses: "One God and Father...who is *in** all" (Eph. 4:6). "Jesus Christ is *in* you" (2 Cor. 13:5). "...His Spirit that dwelleth *in* you" (Rom. 8:11). These three verses reveal that God the Father, the Son, and the Spirit are *in* us. How many Persons, then, are in us? Three, or one? We should not say that three separate Persons are in us, neither should we say that only one Person is in us, but that the Three-in-one is in us. The three Persons of the Godhead are not three Spirits, but one Spirit. The Father is in the Son, and the Son with all His seven wonderful elements is in the Spirit. When this wonderful Holy Spirit comes into us, the Godhead is then dispensed into us. Because the three Persons are in one Spirit, we have the Father, the Son, and the Holy Spirit within us. Later, we will see that the Triune God is in our human spirit to be our spiritual, inner life. This is the very mark of God's economy, and this is the method whereby the Godhead is dispensed into us. The goal of the divine economy is to dispense the Triune God in one Spirit into our human spirit. Hence, we must now focus our whole attention

---

* All italics used in Scripture quotations are ours.

upon living by the Triune God, who dwells within our human spirit. If we are distracted from this, however good and scriptural other things are, we will surely miss the mark of God's economy. The Lord today is recovering His children by causing them to center on this mark of His divine economy.

O Lord Thou art in me as life,
    And everything to me!
Subjective and available,
    Thus I experience Thee.

Chorus
    O Lord, Thou art the Spirit!
    How dear and near to me!
    How I admire Thy marvelous
        Availability!

To all my needs both great and small
    Thou art the rich supply;
So ready and sufficient too
    For me now to apply.

Thy sweet anointing with Thy might
    In weakness doth sustain;
By Thy supply of energy
    My strength Thou dost maintain.

Thy law of life in heart and mind
    My conduct regulates.
The wealth of Thy reality
    My being saturates.

O Thou art ever one with me,
    Unrivaled unity!
One spirit with me all the time
    For all eternity!

Hymn #539 in *Hymns*.

CHAPTER TWO

THE ALL-SUFFICIENT SPIRIT

THE SPIRIT IS THE TRANSMISSION OF GOD

In chapter one we saw that God's economy is to dispense Himself into us by the three Persons of the Godhead. Electricity can be used to illustrate the economy of the Trinity. It includes the source, the current, and the transmission. These seem to be three different kinds of electricity, but in reality they are one. The source, the current, and the transmission are the electricity itself. If the electricity did not exist, neither the source, the current, nor the transmission could exist. As there is one electricity with three different stages, so there is one God with three Persons. At one end is the source or the storage of electricity, while at the other end is the transmission of electricity into our homes. Between the two ends is the current. This is an example of three stages of one and the same thing. God as the Father is the source; God as the Son is the course and the very expression of the Father; and God as the Spirit is the transmission of God into man. Therefore, the Father is the Spirit, the Son is also the Spirit, and the Spirit, of course, is the Spirit. The Father is in the Son, the Son is in the Spirit, and the Spirit is in us as the very transmission of God, transmitting constantly all that God is and has in Christ.

THE SPIRIT IS THE ALL-INCLUSIVE DOSE

In this modern era man has perfected many drugs in the field of medicine. Some drugs are composed of a great number of elements and can be dispensed into one single dose. In just one dosage, some of the elements can destroy germs, others can relax the nerves, and still other elements can nourish and refresh the body. This is an all-inclusive dose. Have we ever realized that the Holy Spirit is the best "dose" in the whole world? Just one dose is enough to meet all our need. All that the Father and the Son are and all They have are in this wonderful Spirit. Consider how many elements are within this dose: God's divine nature, His human nature, His human living with its earthly sufferings, the wonderful effectiveness of His death, His resurrection, His ascension, and His enthronement. Oh, we cannot imagine what kind of dose this is! Yet, praise the Lord, every day we may enjoy it. No scientist or medical doctor on earth could analyze this wonderful dose. This is the economy of God, which is nothing else but God dispensing Himself into us.

It is not a matter of learning doctrines. When I was young, I learned all the doctrines about the various dispensations. I was taught that there were at least seven dispensations. But strictly speaking, there is only one dispensation which we need—the dispensation of God Himself. The sixty-six books of the Scriptures are a full record of this one dispensation—the dispensing of God Himself into us. Oh, that we may partake of Him all the day as the all-inclusive dose in this wonderful Spirit! Let us enjoy God Himself—not these dispensational doctrines.

Are you a weak brother? Here is a dose, a wonderful dose, to strengthen you with might and divine power. Are you a troubled brother? The cure is in the dose. One dose of the Holy Spirit will cure all your troubles.

When I was young, I was taught that we have been crucified with Christ and that I must reckon myself dead. So from morning until evening I was on the alert to reckon myself dead. But the more I did so, the more I became alive. It did not work, because it was the wrong formula. One day, after many years, the Lord opened my eyes to see that the reality of His death is not in my reckoning, but in my enjoyment of the Holy Spirit. This is revealed in Romans 8. Romans 6 gives only the definition, but Romans 8 gives the reality of the death of Christ, because the effectiveness of Christ's death is in the Holy Spirit. The more we fellowship with Christ in the Holy Spirit, the more we will be slain. The dose of the all-inclusive Holy Spirit contains the killing element. There is no need to reckon ourselves dead when we are in the Holy Spirit, because we are enjoying Him as this wonderful dose. Spontaneously, the many germs within us will be killed.

Formerly when I hated a brother, I was told that the "hating I" was crucified, and instead of hating him I should love him. So I tried to reckon myself dead, but it did not work. The more I reckoned myself dead, the more I hated him. Then one day, while fellowshipping with the Lord, I was filled with His Holy Spirit. How the tears flowed! I knew the killing power was within me, killing my hatred and my pride. Automatically, love mingled with tears welled up from my heart for this brother. What was this? This was the killing element in the wonderful dose, the effectiveness of Christ's death in the Spirit.

Within this Spirit of Jesus, there is an all-sufficient supply. The word "supply" in Philippians 1:19 is a special Greek word meaning "the bountiful or all-inclusive supply." The Spirit of Jesus is an all-inclusive supply in which all our needs are met. What do we need? Do we need comfort? No one can truly comfort us—not even our children, our parents, or our dear wives. Real comfort comes from the indwelling Spirit of Jesus. When we fellowship with Jesus in this Spirit and when we live in this wonderful Spirit, we automatically have inward comfort. Regardless of the outward environment, there is inward rest and comfort.

We may say: "I do not know what to do. I need guidance." Living guidance is in the Holy Spirit. When we fellowship with the Lord and walk in the Holy Spirit, we will spontaneously have inward light for guidance. Everything—including guidance—is in the Holy Spirit. Today He is in us as the all-inclusive dose. We need not ask or cry. We only need to take Him, enjoy Him and praise Him.

For example, a sister was in trouble and did not know what to do. Although she had no clear guidance, she went to the Lord and said: "Lord, I praise You that I have no guidance. I praise You that I do not know what to do. I praise You that I am in darkness." What happened? The more she praised, the more she was in the light! Let us do the same thing. When we are weak, let us go to the Lord, saying, "I praise You, Lord, that in this situation I am weak." By contacting Him, we will see what a wonderful Spirit He is, dwelling within us to be the bountiful and all-sufficient supply!

Too many doctrines in Christianity are distracting the Lord's people from the Lord Himself, causing them to miss the mark of God's economy. What is this mark? It is simply the all-inclusive Holy Spirit dwelling in our human spirit. During the whole day, learn how to contact and follow the Holy Spirit. Learn how to fellowship and deal with Him. Christianity teaches us to deal with forms, regulations and doctrines. Even the Scriptures are read in a wrong way, since little or no contact is made with the Holy Spirit in the reading. We merely learn doctrines in black and white letters. We need to read the Scriptures by exercising our spirit to contact the Holy Spirit, not by using our eyes to see the words and exercising our minds merely to understand its teachings. From morning to evening, we must deal with the One dwelling in us, for He is the bountiful supply of the Lord Jesus.

THE SPIRIT IS THE MUTUAL ABODE

John 14:23 says that the Father and the Lord will come to make Their abode with us. What does this mean? Have you ever experienced the Father and the Son coming to make Their abode with you? This is the mark of God's economy which we are considering. This abode is two-sided—the Father and the Son will become our abode, and we will become Their abode. It is a mutual abode. How can this *mutual* abode be possible? Only as we are in the Spirit, just as the Father and the Son are in the Spirit, can we experience this mutual abiding. When we are in the Spirit, we are abiding in the Son and the Father, and at the same time They are abiding in us. Only then will we have an intimate communion and fellowship with the Father and the Son. We will have an inward "talking." We will talk with the Lord, and the Lord will talk with us. These are the practical experiences of the mutual abode.

THE SPIRIT IS THE INNER LIFE AND OUTER CLOTHING

The Lord is also the Spirit of life within us as water that refreshes, strengthens and fills us with the inner life (John 7:37-39).

The Lord as the Holy Spirit is also likened to clothing (In Luke 24:49 of the King James Version, the word "endued" in Greek is "clothed," as translated in the American Standard Version). Clothing indicates power and authority. Today, when anyone is performing an official act of responsibility, he needs a uniform. Suppose we should see a policeman standing on the street in plain clothes, without his uniform. No one would respect him as a policeman. He has lost his authority, because he lacks a uniform. When we see a policeman in uniform while we are driving, we suddenly become very cautious. When he wears his uniform, he is clothed with authority. The Holy Spirit within is the supply of life, and the Holy Spirit without is the uniform of authority. When we are clothed with Him, we have the highest authority in the universe.

After the resurrection, the Lord came to His disciples and breathed on them (John 20:21, 22). He called that very *breath* the "Holy Spirit," because He Himself *is* the Holy Spirit. Whatever comes out of Him must be the Holy Spirit. We know that breath is something of life and something for life. The Lord's breathing of the Holy Spirit into the disciples was the imparting of His Spirit of life to them. From that day of Resurrection all the disciples received the Spirit of life within them. They received the inner drinking of the water of life.

However, at that time they were without power. The uniform was not yet given. Therefore, the Lord told them to wait (Luke 24:49) until He had ascended to the heavens to become enthroned as the Head and the Authority of the universe. It was by His ascension and enthronement that He gained the position to pour Himself down in the Holy Spirit as the authority. On the day of Pentecost the Holy Spirit came down—not as life, but as power (Acts 1:8).

Therefore, on the day of Resurrection, which is the day of life, the Holy Spirit came out of the Lord and entered the disciples as the breath of life. But on the day of Pentecost, which is the day of power, the Holy Spirit came from the ascended and enthroned Head and equipped the disciples with authority for service. This is the Holy Spirit of power as the uniform.

Suppose a policeman is preparing to go on duty. What does he usually do before beginning his work? Early in the morning he drinks several cups of some beverage in order to refresh and strengthen himself. But will he, by filling up with this beverage, be *qualified* to perform his duty as a policeman? If he merely goes out into the street without the uniform, exclaiming, "I'm full; now I am a policeman," nobody would respect him. They would say that he is crazy. Though he is a real policeman, yet without the uniform he lacks authority. But when he puts on the uniform, he is thus equipped with the power of authority. Then, when he goes out on the street, everyone respects him as a man with the authority of the local police. We cannot despise this uniform. This uniform represents the authority of the government. On the other hand, if the policeman drank nothing in the morning, he would be weak. He could put on his uniform and exercise his position of authority, but he would have no inward strength and refreshment.

Some Christians who are filled within are without the uniform, while other Christians who wear a proper uniform are empty within. We need both the inward filling and the outward equipping. We need the Holy Spirit of the Resurrection Day as life "within" us and the Holy Spirit of the Pentecostal Day as power "upon" us. The filling of the Holy Spirit is necessary inwardly; the clothing of the Holy Spirit is also necessary outwardly. If we have both aspects, we will experience the blessed mingling of the Holy Spirit within and without. And who is the Spirit? Remember that the Spirit is the very reality of the Triune God. As we are filled and clothed with the Holy Spirit, we are mingled with the Triune God. This is the mark of God's economy.

Oh, let us pay our attention to this mark of God's economy and not to mere doctrine! Some try to argue about doctrines. They say, "What about the rapture?" Many Christians are troubled about post-rapture, pre-rapture, partial rapture or something else. Once I told a dear brother, "As long as you love the Lord and live by Him, when He comes back you will be raptured. That is good enough!" Let us forget about doctrines and learn to love Him. Aim at the mark of His economy, deal with the living Christ in the Holy Spirit and be filled and clothed with Him.

Some argue about eternal security, but the real security is simply Christ Himself, not the teaching of eternal security. As long as we have Christ, we have security. If we do not have Christ, we do not have security. The doctrine of eternal security is not Christ. Doctrine only works divisions among the Lord's children. If we love Christ, walk by the living Spirit and do not emphasize the doctrines, we will be one with all saints. The more we talk about doctrines, the more we will quarrel. Today, while we talk about the Holy Spirit, the wonderful dose, we all say, "Amen! Hallelujah!" But tomorrow, if we talk about eternal security, some will say, "I'm sorry, I cannot agree." Immediately we will be divided, and this means we have missed the mark. We will be teaching things which only raise questions rather than concentrating our full attention upon the mark of God's economy. What is the mark? It is the Father in the Son, and the Son in the Holy Spirit, and the Holy Spirit in us.

Others are arguing about baptism. For instance, some try to convince others by insisting on sprinkling. Again, this is a matter of doctrine and not a matter of the Spirit of the living Christ. We must learn to grasp one thing and to be grasped by one thing—Christ Himself. We must learn how to grasp Christ in the Holy Spirit and be grasped by the Holy Spirit. Although we can certainly receive help from doctrine, the main center of God's economy is not doctrine, but the living One in the Holy Spirit.

THE SPIRIT IS THE LIFE-GIVING, LIBERATING, TRANSFORMING SPIRIT

If we contact this living One in the wonderful Holy Spirit throughout the whole day, three things will happen within. First, the life-giving Spirit will impart life (2 Cor. 3:6). Whenever we contact this wonderful Spirit, we will have the inner refreshing, the inner strengthening, the inner satisfying and the inner enlightening. These are indications that Christ as life is being imparted more and more into us. We may have been a Christian for more than eighty years, yet we still need the Christ of God as the life-giving Spirit, imparting Himself into us, refreshing us, strengthening us, satisfying us, enlightening us and filling us. This wonderful Spirit is within us to impart Christ as our bountiful supply.

Next, the Holy Spirit will continually liberate us (2 Cor. 3:17). Many oppressions and depressions of the day tend to weaken us. Sometimes a person's long face will depress us. Sometimes your wife may not feel well, and when you arrive home from work she may become unhappy with you. Later, if you should come to a meeting, you will appear with a long face. People will ask, "What happened to you, brother?" And you will say, "Nothing!" You dare not tell them that your wife has influenced you by her behavior. Such a little matter can suppress and depress you. However, if you contact the living Christ within you, He will immediately liberate you. You will be transcendent far above your wife, and all the depression will be under your feet! You will be liberated to the throne in the third heaven. Many times when I was prepared to come to a ministry meeting, something would happen! But I learned the lesson. I said, "Lord, I am in the heavens; I will not be disturbed by all these things." If we are in the Holy Spirit, we will be transcendent, because in this wonderful Spirit are the elements of ascension and transcendency. When we are in Him, these elements in the Spirit will liberate us all the day.

Finally, while He imparts life and liberates us, the Holy Spirit also transforms us. 2 Corinthians 3:18, according to the proper translation, says: "We all, with unveiled face beholding and reflecting as a mirror the glory of the Lord, are transformed into the same image from glory to glory, even as from the Lord the Spirit." In this verse, the word "transformed" is rendered as "changed" in the King James Version, but in the Greek it is the same word as in Romans 12:2, "*transformed* by the renewing of your mind." To be transformed does not merely mean to be changed outwardly, but changed both in nature within and in form without. As we behold and reflect as a mirror the glory of the Lord, we are transformed into the

Lord's image from one stage of glory to another. When a mirror beholds anything, it reflects what it beholds. But if a mirror is veiled, its face is not open; even if it beholds an object, it cannot reflect it. If we are an open mirror, we will reflect Christ by beholding Him. This is the process of transformation. The Lord is the Spirit transforming us within. Although we are so natural and even sinful, the Spirit transforms our natural image into His glorious image. During the whole day, if we live in the Spirit, He will transform us by renewing our mind, our emotion and our will. By saturating our mind, emotion and will with Himself, He will occupy all the inward parts of our being. Our love, our hatred, our desires, our choices and our decisions will bear His image. We will be transformed into His image from glory to glory—that is, today we are transformed in the first stage of glory, tomorrow we will be transformed in the second stage of glory, and the next day in the third stage. Every day the glory will be increased.

The economy of God and the aim of His economy is that God is going to dispense Himself into us and mingle us with Himself in His glory. Then we can express Him. Let us be faithful to this aim, let us hold fast to this mark, and let us go on to reach this goal.

Chapter Three

THE RESIDENCE OF THE DIVINE SPIRIT

In John 3:6 we read: "That which is born of the Spirit is spirit." This verse speaks of two distinct "spirits": one is capitalized and the other is not. The first occurrence of the word refers to the Holy Spirit of God, and the second to the human spirit of man. That which is born of the Holy Spirit is the human spirit. Another verse showing these two "spirits" is John 4:24: "God is a Spirit: and they that worship him must worship in spirit." Again, the first "Spirit" is capitalized and the second is not. We must worship God, who is the Spirit, in our human spirit. Romans 8:16 further confirms the existence of two spirits: "The Spirit himself beareth witness with our spirit, that we are children of God." The pronoun "our" definitely designates the human spirit and removes any ground to doubt the reality of both the divine Spirit and the human spirit.

In Romans 8:9, 10 we read: "...the Spirit of God dwelleth in you...And if Christ is in you, the body is dead...but the spirit is life." The King James Version capitalizes "spirit" in verse 10, but the better translations, such as the American Standard Version, render "spirit" here with a small letter "s." Why do we point this out? It is because Christians have very little knowledge about man's spirit. Much attention is given to the Holy Spirit, but the human spirit, the residence and dwelling place of the Holy Spirit, is almost entirely neglected. Suppose someone wants to visit me. He must first find where I live. If he cannot locate my home, he will have to forfeit his visit. Although there is much talk about the Holy Spirit, yet we do not know where He dwells. Romans 8:9 refers without a doubt to the Holy Spirit, but verse 10 speaks of the human spirit. "...The *body* is dead...but the *spirit* is life." Of course, the Holy Spirit cannot be compared with our body. The comparison must be between the human body and the human spirit—not between the human body and the Holy Spirit.

The Apostle Paul said: "For God is my witness, whom I serve in *my* spirit in the gospel of his Son" (Rom. 1:9). Our usual thought is that God is served in the Holy Spirit, but here is a verse declaring that God is served in our human spirit. In Galatians 5:16, the phrase "walk in the Spirit" contains the definite article "the" and capitalizes "Spirit," but the Greek interlinear text omits both the article and the capital. Many Christians, due to the rendering of the King James Version, think this verse means to walk in the Holy Spirit, but according to the Greek text it means to walk in our spirit. We would profit by comparing translations to find the correct meaning. In many verses the word "spirit" should not be capitalized.

Bible translators have found it very difficult to decide whether "spirit" in some passages refers to the Holy Spirit or the human spirit. The reason for this difficulty is that in the believer the Holy Spirit and the human spirit are mingled together as one spirit! "He that is joined unto the Lord is one spirit" (1 Cor. 6:17). We are one spirit with the Lord, but one which is clearly mingled with the Holy Spirit. Such a mingled spirit makes it difficult for anyone to say whether this is the Holy Spirit or the human spirit. The two are mingled as one. We may say it is the Holy Spirit, and yet we can also say it is the human spirit of the saints. Sometimes we make a beverage by mingling two kinds of juices—pineapple and grapefruit. After it is mixed it is difficult to tell what kind of juice it is. Is it pineapple or is it grapefruit? We would have to call it pineapple-grapefruit. In the New Testament it is wonderful to see that the two spirits, the Holy Spirit mingled with our spirit, are one spirit.

LOCATING THE HUMAN SPIRIT

In the first chapter we saw that God the Father is in us (Eph. 4:6), Christ is in us (2 Cor. 13:5), and the Holy Spirit is in us (Rom. 8:11). All three Persons of the Triune God are in us. But where within us is the Triune God? In what part? It is so clear, beyond any ground of argument, that Christ today is in our spirit, and we have the Scriptures that confirm this fact. We should not be so vague, like many who say, "Oh, the Lord is in you and the Lord is in me." The last verse of 2 Timothy definitely states that Christ is in our spirit. "The Lord be with thy spirit" (2 Tim. 4:22). In order for Christ to be in our spirit, He must first be Spirit; next, we must have a spirit; finally, these two spirits must be mingled as one spirit. If the Lord is not the Spirit, how could He be in our spirit, and how could we be one spirit with Him?

In order to locate the human spirit, we need to divide the soul from the spirit. "For the word of God is living, and active, and sharper than any two-edged sword, and piercing even to the dividing of soul and spirit, of both joints and marrow, and quick to discern the thoughts and intents of the heart" (Heb. 4:12). God's word is a sharp sword to pierce our being, to divide our soul from our spirit.

For example, we are told in 1 Corinthians 3 that we are the temple of God. God's temple according to the Old Testament is portrayed in three parts: the first is the outer court, the second is the holy place, and the third is the Holiest of all, the Most Holy place.

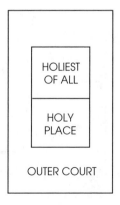

We know that God was in His temple, but in what part?
Was He in the outer court or in the holy place? No. He was in
the Holiest of all. There in the Holiest of all dwelt the
Shekinah presence of God. In the *outer court* was the altar,
which is a type of the cross, and directly behind the altar was
the laver, which in type is the work of the Holy Spirit. The
holy place included the showbread table, the candlestick, and
the incense altar. But what was in the *Holiest of all?* The ark
which typifies Christ! Therefore, Christ was in the Holiest of
all, and God's presence, the Shekinah glory of God, was there
also.

The Scriptures point out that we too are the temple (1 Cor.
3:16). We as tripartite beings are also composed of three
parts—the body, the soul, and the spirit. But in which part of
our being does the Triune God dwell? 2 Timothy 4:22 states
clearly that the Lord is in our spirit. Our spirit is the very
Holiest of all. The typology of the Old Testament temple presents a very clear picture. Christ and God's presence are in the
Holiest of all. Today this type of the temple of God is fulfilled
in us. We are of three parts: our body corresponds to the outer
court, our soul to the holy place, and our human spirit to the
Holiest of all, which is the very residence of Christ and God's
presence. This is illustrated in the following diagram:

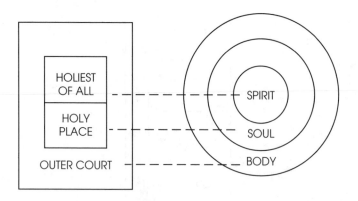

"Having therefore, brethren, boldness to enter into the holiest by the blood of Jesus" (Heb. 10:19 A.V.). What is "the holiest" for us to enter today while we are here on earth? Look at the above diagram. Our human spirit is the Holiest of all which is God's residence, the very chamber in which God and Christ dwell. If we would find God and Christ, there is no need for us to go to heaven. God in Christ is so available, for He is in our spirit.

DIVIDING THE SOUL FROM THE HUMAN SPIRIT

For this reason we have to divide our soul from our spirit (Heb. 4:12). If we are unable to divide the soul from the spirit, we simply cannot contact the Lord. Look at the picture. If the high priest was unable to locate the Holiest of all, his efforts to contact God would only have ended in failure. First, he had to enter the outer court, and from the outer court he had to enter the holy place, and from the holy place he would finally enter the Holiest of all. There he would meet God and see the Shekinah glory of God's presence.

We must learn to discern our spirit from our soul. The soul conceals and covers the spirit, just as the bones conceal the marrow. It is easy to see the bones, but not the marrow hidden within. If we are going to get the marrow, we have to break the bones. Sometimes the marrow has to be scraped from the bones. Oh, how our spirit sticks to our soul! Our spirit is hidden and concealed within it. The soul is easily recognized, but the spirit is difficult to know. We know a little about the Holy Spirit, but we do not know the human spirit. Why? Because the human spirit is concealed in the soul. This is why the soul needs to be broken, and just as the joints are the strongest part of the bones, so our soul is very strong. We have a spirit, but our soul covers it up. God's Word as a sharp sword must pierce our soul in order to break it away from the spirit.

"There remaineth therefore a sabbath rest for the people of God. Let us therefore give diligence to enter into that rest, that no man fall after the same example of disobedience" (Heb. 4:9, 11). What is this rest? We have to look at another type in the Old Testament to discover its meaning. After the

Israelites were delivered and saved from the land of Egypt, they were brought into the wilderness with the intention that they should go on into the land of Canaan. The land of Canaan was their land of rest, a type of the all-inclusive Christ. Christ is the good land of Canaan, and He is our Rest. If we are going to enter into the rest, we must enter into Christ. But where is Christ today? We answer that He is in our spirit. The Israelites, who were delivered out of Egypt, instead of going on into Canaan, wandered for many years in the wilderness. What does this typify? It means that many Christians after being saved are simply wandering in the soul. The reason the book to the Hebrews was written is that many Hebrew Christians were saved, but they were wandering in their soul. They would not press on from the wilderness into the good land—that is, into Christ who dwelt in their spirit. We must not continue to wander in our soul, but press on to enter into our spirit, where Christ is our rest.

Let us illustrate further by the following diagram:

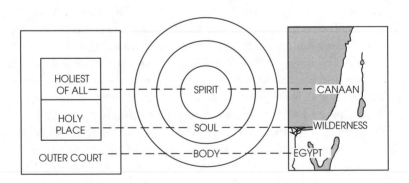

In ancient times all the people of Israel had access to the outer court, but only the priests could enter the holy place. Furthermore, into the Holiest of all only one, the High Priest, could enter, and that only once a year. Moreover, of all the

Israelites who were saved and brought out of Egypt into the wilderness, very few went on into the good land of Canaan.

Even though we may have been saved for years, we must ask ourselves whether we are presently a Christian living in the body, in the soul, or in the spirit. Are we now in Egypt, in the wilderness, or in the good land of Canaan? Ask the Lord and search yourself in order to be clear where you are. Frankly, many Christians are wandering all day in the soul, that is, in the wilderness. In the morning they have smiling faces, but by afternoon they are sorrowful with long faces. Yesterday, it seems they were in the heavens, but today they are down. They are wandering in the soul, the wilderness, without rest, circling in the same rut day after day. They may have been following the Lord for twenty years, but are still going in circles, just as the people of Israel, who wandered for thirty-eight years with no improvement and no progress. Why? Because they are in the soul. When we are in the soul, we are in the wilderness.

This is why the writer to the Hebrews emphasized the need to divide the soul from the spirit. The Word of God must pierce us so that we may know how to press on from the soul into the good land and the Holiest place of our human spirit. A soulish believer is one wandering in the wilderness of the soul, where there is no rest.

The High Priest had to pass through the veil in order to enter into the Holiest of all; so the veil, which typifies the flesh (Heb. 10:20), must be riven and broken. Furthermore, the people of Israel had to cross the river of Jordan in order to enter the good land. Under the waters of the Jordan they buried twelve stones, representing the twelve tribes of Israel, and another twelve stones, representing the resurrected Israelites, were brought over into the good land. The old generation of Israel was buried in the death-waters of the Jordan River. All of this typifies that the natural man, the soulish life, or the old nature must be broken as the veil and buried as the old man. Then we can enter into the Holiest of all and into the good land in order to enjoy Christ as our rest.

DISTRACTIONS FROM THE HUMAN SPIRIT

These pictures will help us to realize that God's economy is the Triune God in our human spirit. This Triune God in the one Spirit has taken our spirit as His residence and His dwelling place. So we must learn to discern our spirit from our soul. The problem is that we Christians are full of many natural thoughts. After we have been saved, we think that we have to be good and to do good. But God, in His economy, intends to work Himself into us as our life and as everything to us. We must forget everything else and concentrate upon the indwelling Christ in our spirit. We must not be distracted from the aim and mark of this indwelling Christ. Forget about being good and doing good deeds. Drop all those good things and enter the Holiest of all. Many Christians are busily working in the outer court. They do not know that God's intention for them is to go into the Holiest of all where they can contact God, be filled with God, be occupied with God, be one with God in everything and have God as their all. Discern your spirit and fellowship with this indwelling One. Let Him take over and possess you.

Another religious distraction is that after we are saved we feel that we are weak, that we need strength and power. Consequently, we pray that the Holy Spirit might be poured upon us that we might be made strong and powerful. Although there is some ground for us to do this, yet the main line of God's economy is that we follow Him, not in this outward empowering, but in our spirit where the Triune God dwells. Therefore, the most vital thing is for us to know our spirit and to deny our soul. We need to reject our soul and to walk after our spirit, because the Triune God is in our spirit. This mark of God's economy is missed by most Christians—even the seeking ones!

Again we ask, where is this Triune God today? Praise the Lord, this wonderful One, the Triune God, is today in our spirit! We have Him! Yes, we have Him in our spirit! This wonderful, all-inclusive Spirit is in us! If we are a believer, we have the Triune God in our human spirit. Our need, today, is to discern our spirit from our soul. When we know the proper way to discern the spirit from the soul, we will hit the mark of contacting this Triune God.

In the mechanics of a radio there is a receiver, a receiving organ. When we tune the radio accurately, the electric wave in the air will hit that receiver. Today the Triune God is the spiritual electricity. He is the electric wave throughout the universe, and we are the radio. What is the receiver within us? It is our human spirit. We tune our human spirit rightly when we have a broken and contrite spirit, when we are repentant before God and open unto Him. If we have such a spirit, the Triune God, who is the wonderful Spirit and who is the spiritual electricity, will immediately hit our spirit! All we need to know is how to tune the receiver, how to tune our human spirit, discerning the spirit from all other things such as our thinking, our emotions and our choices. When we discern our spirit from all these soulish things, then we will know how to contact the divine Spirit, who is the wonderful, all-inclusive Spirit of the Triune God. Then we will know the Lord's Word as the sharp sword, piercing to divide our soul from our spirit, and we will realize how to experience, enjoy, and partake of the indwelling Christ all the time.

CHAPTER FOUR

THE KEY TO THE INDWELLING SPIRIT

In more than twenty translations of the New Testament there is a difference in the way "spirit" is written. In some translations the word is capitalized in certain instances, while in the same instances in other translations it is not. For example, the translators of the King James Version capitalized the word "spirit" in Romans 8:2, "the law of the Spirit," but the text of one Greek interlinear does *not* capitalize the word "spirit" in this verse. "Spirit" is capitalized in verse 4 in the King James Version—"who walk...after the Spirit"—but the same Greek interlinear text does *not* capitalize it. Again, in verse 5—"they that are after the Spirit"—the King James Version capitalizes "spirit," whereas the text of this Greek interlinear does not capitalize the word.

What is the reason for such conflicting translations? It is difficult for any translator to decide whether "spirit" is referring to the Holy Spirit or the human spirit in passages such as these. Since our spirit has been mingled together with the Holy Spirit, the two spirits are mingled as one spirit (1 Cor. 6:17). Therefore, one may assert that this spirit is the human spirit, while another may say this Spirit is the Holy Spirit. Of course, the context of some passages makes it clear that the reference is to the Holy Spirit, while in other passages, the human spirit.

"And if Christ be in you, the body is dead because of sin, but the *spirit* is life because of righteousness." The context of this verse, Romans 8:10, clearly indicates that here the spirit is *not* the Holy Spirit, because it is compared with the body. We cannot compare the Holy Spirit with our body. It is our human spirit which the Apostle was comparing with our body.

What is the meaning of this verse? Originally, our body was dead because of sin. Now Christ is in us, and though our sinful body is still dead because of sin, yet our spirit is alive and full of life because of righteousness. Therefore, the "spirit" mentioned here in this verse is not the Holy Spirit, but the human spirit, which is compared with the human body.

In another verse, Romans 8:11, it is obvious that reference is made to the Spirit *of God*. What follows the phrase, "the Spirit *of him*," defines whose Spirit it is. "But if the Spirit of him that raised up Jesus from the dead dwelleth in you, he that raised up Christ Jesus from the dead shall give life also to your mortal bodies through his Spirit that dwelleth in you." Verse 10 tells us that though Christ is in us, our body is still dead because of sin. However, verse 11 declares that our weak, mortal bodies, due to Christ's indwelling, will also be quickened, revived and strengthened. Because Christ is living in us, even our mortal bodies which are dead because of sin could be quickened and revived by the divine Spirit who is dwelling within our spirit. The indwelling Spirit makes us alive not only in our spirit, but eventually also in our body.

THE HUMAN SPIRIT AS THE KEY

Why are we emphasizing the difference between the Holy Spirit and the human spirit? It is because our greatest problem is that we do not know the indwelling Spirit or realize that the human spirit is the very dwelling place of the Holy Spirit; neither do we know that these two spirits are being mingled together as one Spirit. This is a pity! It is the mark of God's economy, and many Christians are missing this mark. It is like a house that is inaccessible because the key is missing. Only the key will open the house to us that we may enjoy everything in it. For centuries the enemy has covered the key. What is the key? It is that *our human spirit is the dwelling place* of the Holy Spirit, and that our human spirit is one with the wonderful Holy Spirit.

The Word of God is living and sharp, even sharper than a two-edged sword, piercing to divide asunder the soul and the spirit. For more than thirty years, I tried to understand why this word was written and why it was written in Hebrews chapter four. The Lord has revealed the reason. The book of Hebrews is encouraging us to press on from the wilderness into the good land, from the wandering stage to the resting stage in the all-inclusive Christ. At that time, the Hebrew Christians were in danger of drifting away from Christ into Judaism, which is like returning to the land of Egypt. They had been delivered out of Judaism and intended to enter into the good land of rest, but they were wandering midway between Judaism and Christ. The Epistle to the Hebrews was written to encourage them to press beyond the wandering stage by taking Christ as their all-inclusive life and rest.

Hebrews also refers to the Holiest of all. Again, for many years I could not understand what is the Holiest of all. Eventually I was helped by the Lord to realize that the Holiest of all is, in a sense, our very spirit. Today our human spirit is the Holiest of all. The three parts of the temple correspond to the three parts of man—body, soul and spirit. The inmost part of the temple, the Holiest of all, indicates the inmost part of our being, the human spirit. Just as the ark, the type of Christ, was in the Holiest of all, so is Christ in our spirit today. Our human spirit, therefore, is the Holiest of all where we can contact God. If we cannot discern our spirit, we cannot locate the Holiest of all.

Furthermore, we must be very clear that today the Triune God has completed everything—the creation, the incarnation and the life and sufferings on earth; He has gone into death and passed through death; He has resurrected, ascended into heaven, and has been enthroned. Everything has been attained by the wonderful Triune God, and all these realities are in the Holy Spirit, who has come into us. The point is that this Holy Spirit has been dispensed into our human spirit, which is now the residence of God. Our spirit is the organ to receive God and to contain Him. If we are going to contact this wonderful Spirit, we must know our spirit. If you are going to contact me, you must know where I live. Hebrews 4:12 was written to encourage us to press on into the Holiest of all, which is our spirit. If we do not know how to discern our spirit, we cannot locate the Holiest of all, the place where the Lord dwells today. God's economy is to dispense Himself into us, and the very place where He dispenses Himself is our spirit. When we are able to discern our spirit and to exercise our spirit to contact the Lord, we can then be permeated and saturated with the Lord and be transformed into His image.

DISTRACTIONS FROM THE KEY

(1) Good

The enemy tries to frustrate us from discerning our spirit, and soon after we are saved he does this by helping us make a decision to do good. No one is exempt from this subtle suggestion. Even this morning some have prayed, "Lord, I want to do Your will; I want to please You; I will try my best to do the things that satisfy You." This sounds like a good prayer, but it is not from the Lord. It comes from the enemy. Whenever we have such good intentions, we must jump up and tell Satan to depart from us. In my Christian dictionary there is not such a word as "evil," nor is there such a word as "good"! From the beginning to the end my Christian dictionary contains only one word—"Christ"! I understand neither good nor evil. I do not want help to do good; I only want Christ!

Now you can understand the Lord's words, "Abide in me, and I in you; he that abideth in me, and I in him, the same beareth much fruit." Here there is nothing of self-effort, only abiding in the indwelling One, and allowing Him to abide in us; then all the riches of Christ will be wrought out through us. Fruit-bearing is simply the outworking of the indwelling Christ. We should say, "I do not know this and I do not know that. I only know one thing: I am a branch, and He is the vine; I have to abide in Him, and let Him abide in me." Spontaneously we will bear fruit. This is the missing key. Trying to do good is a real temptation and a great distraction from experiencing Christ.

(2) Doctrines

Doctrines form another device used by the enemy to distract the seeking ones from Christ. Through the centuries, doctrines such as eternal security, dispensations, predestination, absolute grace, etc., have been much used by the enemy to distract Christians from the living Christ. I knew some Christians who were so familiar with the Bible that one of them was even called the "living concordance." If you could not find a certain portion in the Scriptures, they could tell you immediately the book, chapter, and verse. But I can testify that they knew very little about contacting Christ as their life. To possess the knowledge of the Scriptures is one thing, but to know the living One revealed by the Scriptures is quite another. Christ must be contacted through the Scriptures. But it is regrettable that so many Christians have the Scriptures only in their hand and in their memory, with very little of Christ in their spirit. The Mosaic law was to bring people to Christ and keep them for Christ. It was to help people to know Christ; but many merely kept the law and ignored Christ. Therefore, the law was misused. Today, the problem remains unchanged. The same principle applies to all the teachings and doctrines of the Scriptures. Doctrines are the means to experience Christ, but Christians use the doctrines and knowledge to replace Him.

(3) Gifts

Another thing which the enemy utilizes is the matter of spiritual gifts. A proper understanding of the gifts is necessary in order to see how they are related to God's economy. This applies to all gifts. Many gifted persons give too much attention to their gifts and, more or less, neglect the indwelling Christ. The indwelling Christ is the mark of God's economy, and all the gifts are for this. Many know how to speak in tongues and how to have healing, but they do not know how to discern the spirit and contact Christ. Although I am not speaking against any gift, I am against one thing—that is, paying full attention to the gifts and ignoring the discernment of the spirit in order to contact Christ. This is definitely wrong.

The book of Romans allots very little ground to the gifts. Romans is a general sketch of the Christian life and walk, and in such a sketch not much reference is made to gifts. Of sixteen chapters, only chapter 12 speaks something about them, and if the whole twelfth chapter is read, we will see that not only the gift of prophecy is mentioned, but even the

gifts of showing mercy and of giving material things are listed
(Rom. 12:5-8). The gifts mentioned here result from the living
Christ experienced as grace in each believer. Not all Christians have the gift of prophecy. It is just one of many gifts.
Although we are not trying to oppose any gifts, nevertheless,
we must give proper proportion to every gift; otherwise, we
will be unbalanced.

Gifts are also mentioned in 1 Corinthians 12 and 14. The
Corinthian believers had all the gifts and were behind in
none of them (1 Cor. 1:7). Yet, though the Corinthians had all
the gifts, their spiritual condition was described as carnal
and immature (1 Cor. 3:1). We may have the gifts, yet remain
childish and carnal. There is no doubt we can receive help
from these gifts, but we need to learn something more. Signs
and wisdom are gifts (1 Cor. 1:22), but the Apostle preached
"Christ crucified" and "Christ, the power of God and the
wisdom of God." The Apostle's only intention was to minister
Christ as the power and the wisdom—not the manifestations
of the gifts and signs. The gifts are a help, but they are not
the goal and the mark. The mark is the indwelling Christ.
The gifts should only help us to realize this mark.

First Corinthians 12 mentions spiritual gifts, including
speaking in tongues, but at the end of the chapter Paul mentions "the more excellent way." The Greek text expresses it
even more strongly: "the *most* excellent way." What is the
most excellent way? Chapter 13 is the continuation of this
verse: If we speak with all the tongues of men and angels and
have not love, we are merely sounding brass. We hear only a
sound, but we do not see the life! Love is the expression of
life. This proves that tongues, strictly speaking, are not a
matter of life. To speak in tongues without considering the
life is to become sounding brass. Many people who speak fre-
quently in tongues are very shallow and immature in their
Christian life.

In chapter 14, the Apostle encourages us rather to exercise
our spirit for the spiritual profit of the church. This is the conclusion of the whole chapter. Even though Paul exceeded
others in tongues, yet he would rather speak five intelligi-
ble words in the meetings than 10,000 words in tongues

(vv. 18, 19). The Apostle in these chapters manifests a somewhat negative attitude toward speaking in tongues. Rather than encouraging the practice of the gifts, he adjusts the Corinthians with some corrective instruction. Therefore, we must conclude that all the gifts are for the experience of Christ and must be used in proper proportion.

The key to God's economy is Christ as everything wrought into our spirit. Of course, we need certain teachings and certain gifts to help us to realize the mark. But we must not allow the doctrines and gifts to replace this mark. The mark is neither the teachings nor the gifts, but Christ, who is the living Spirit, indwelling our spirit. With some, a gift may be needed to help them to realize this mark. Not all need the same gift. While some may need the gift of prophecy, others may need the gift of speaking in tongues. Some may need the gift of healing, while others need certain doctrines. Many people are drawn to Christ through certain teachings. But let us be clear that the indwelling Christ in our spirit is the key to God's economy. We must give our full attention to this key. Actually, there is no need to give special attention to any kind of teaching or gift if the indwelling Christ is already realized in our spirit.

The old servant of Abraham was sent with a number of gifts to obtain a wife for Isaac. All these gifts helped Rebecca to realize that she must go to meet Isaac. This is the true place of the gifts. But after Rebecca received the gifts, she seemed to forget all about them and said: "I will go to Isaac! I will not be satisfied to remain here enjoying these gifts and yet forget about Isaac. I will go on to meet my bridegroom." After Rebecca married Isaac, there is no further mention of these gifts. Day by day Rebecca just enjoyed living with Isaac. Christ is much better than speaking in tongues, much better than prophecy, much better than everything else!

With the key in my hand, I can open all the doors and enjoy the entire house. If I have no key, I must see the locksmith; but if I have a key, the services of the locksmith are not required. The real need is the key, not the locksmith; and just as the locksmith is not needed when I have the key, so the gifts and the teachings are not needed when we realize the indwelling Christ in our spirit.

Some may require certain teachings and gifts in order to find the key; but, praise the Lord, as long as the key is in our hand to realize Christ, let us forget the teachings and gifts. Let us give our full attention to discerning our spirit, contacting the living Christ, and fellowshipping with Him. In order for us to obtain the key God has proportioned certain gifts and teachings. We can praise the Lord for this mercy, but we must be careful. We must not give so much attention to the locksmith that we go to him every day. As long as the key is obtained, thank the locksmith and leave him! Use the key to come into the building and discover its riches. Day by day learn to know this wonderful Triune God, the unsearchable Christ, the all-inclusive Holy Spirit, who is now in our spirit. We have the key when we discern our spirit. We have the key! Whatever we need of Christ, we have by exercising our spirit to contact Him. This is the mark of God's economy. Although the Lord grants us teachings and gifts, He Himself is the goal, the complete and all-inclusive One. Let us not settle with anything less than Himself. The aim of God's economy is for the all-inclusive Christ to indwell our spirit. All during the day we must seek to return into our spirit, discern our spirit and contact Christ as everything. Then we have the key to the proper and normal Christian life.

CHAPTER FIVE

THE PERSONS OF GOD AND
THE PARTS OF MAN

"And even if our gospel is veiled, it is veiled in them that
perish: in whom the god of this world (or age) hath blinded
the minds of the unbelieving, that the light of the gospel of
the glory of Christ, who is the image of God, should not
dawn upon them. For we preach not ourselves, but Christ
Jesus as Lord, and ourselves as your servants for Jesus'
sake. Seeing it is God, that said, Light shall shine out of
darkness, who shined in our hearts, to give the light of the
knowledge of the glory of God in the face of Jesus Christ.
But we have this treasure in earthen vessels, that the ex-
ceeding greatness of the power may be of God, and not from
ourselves" (2 Cor. 4:3-7).

These verses tell us that Satan, the god of this age, blinds
the minds of the unbelievers, lest "the light of the gospel of
the glory of Christ" should shine into them. The enemy is
afraid of the shining of "the gospel of the glory" of such a
Christ. The "gospel of the glory of Christ" in verse 4 corresponds to the "knowledge of the glory of God" in verse 6. The
"treasure" is the very God in Christ who has shined Himself
into us, the earthen vessels.

We have seen the economy of God and the mark of His
economy. We have pointed out that the main thing in the
economy of God is that God intends to work Himself into us.
He works Himself into our different parts through His different Persons. If we read the Scriptures carefully, we will
realize that this is the main thing. I have such a burden that
I could say this to the Lord's children hundreds of times, yes,
thousands of times: in the whole universe God's intention is
nothing other than to work Himself into man.

For what purpose did God create man? Only that man might be His container. I like to use this word "container" because it is clearer than the word "vessel." It is clearly seen in Romans 9:21, 23 and 2 Corinthians 4:7, that God created us to be His containers in order to contain Himself. We are only empty containers, and God intends to be our only content. To illustrate, bottles are necessary to contain beverages, and light bulbs are necessary to contain electricity. If we look at the bottles made for beverages, or the light bulbs made for electricity, we will realize that these "peculiar" containers are quite specific articles; they were made for a particular use. We people are also "peculiar" containers, for we too were made for a specific purpose. The bulbs once made must now contain electricity; otherwise, they would be meaningless and good for nothing. Likewise, if the bottles never contain a beverage, they also would become meaningless. Man was made purposely to contain God. If we do not contain God and know God as our content, we are a senseless contradiction.

Regardless of how much education we may obtain, what kind of position we may have, or how much wealth we may possess, we are still meaningless, since we were purposely made as a container to contain God as our sole content. As containers, we must receive God into our being. Although this word may seem simple, it is the exact word needed to point out the main thought of the whole Scriptures. The basic teaching of the whole Scriptures is simply this: God is the very content, and we are the containers made to receive this content. We must contain God and be filled with God.

THE FATHER, THE SON, AND THE SPIRIT

In order that God may put Himself into us as our content, He must exist in three Persons. We can never adequately understand the mystery of God's three Persons. We are told clearly in several places in the Scriptures that God is only one God. First Corinthians 8:4, 6 and 1 Timothy 2:5 declare this. But in the first chapter of Genesis the pronoun used for God is not the singular "I," but the plural "we."

Let *us* read Genesis 1:26 and 27. "Let *us* make man in *our* image, after *our* likeness...God created man in *his* own image." In verse 26 it says, "in *our* image," while in the following verse it says "in *his* image." Please tell me, is God singular or plural? Who can explain this? God Himself used the plural pronoun for Himself: "Let *us* make man in *our* image." But if you say God is more than one, you are a heretic, because the Bible tells us God is only one. In the whole universe there is not more than one God. Why, then, if God is only one, is the plural pronoun used?

Everyone who is familiar with Hebrew can tell us that the word "God" in Genesis 1 is in the plural number. The Hebrew word for God in the first verse, "In the beginning God created," is *Elohim,* which is in plural number. However, the word "created" in Hebrew is a predicate in the singular number. This is very strange. The grammatical composition of this verse is a subject in the plural number, but a verb in the singular number. No one can argue with this; it is proven by the Hebrew. Then, I ask, is God one or three?

Now let us read Isaiah 9:6. "For unto us a child is born, unto us a son is given...his name shall be called...Mighty God, Everlasting Father." It does not say mighty man, but Mighty God. A little child is called the Mighty God. All Christians agree with the prophecy of this verse. The child mentioned here refers to the child born in the manger at Bethlehem, who is not only named the Mighty God, but also the Everlasting Father. As a child born to us, He is called the Mighty God; and as a son given to us, He is called the Everlasting Father (or the Father of Eternity). This is very strange. When the *child* is called the Mighty God, is He the child or God? And, when the *son* is called the Everlasting Father, is He the Son or the Father? If you try to figure it out, you cannot do it. You must take it as a fact, unless, of course, you do not believe the Scriptures. If you believe the authority of the Scriptures, you must accept the fact that since the child is called the Mighty God, it means the child *is* the Mighty God; and since the Son is called the Father, it means the Son *is* the Father. If the child is not the Mighty God, how could the child be called the Mighty God? And if the Son is not the Father, how could the Son be called the Father? Then, how many Gods do we have? We have only one God, because the child Jesus is the Mighty God, and the Son is the Everlasting Father.

Furthermore, 2 Corinthians 3:17 says, "Now the Lord is the Spirit." According to our understanding, who is the Lord? We all agree that the Lord is Jesus Christ. But it says the Lord is *the Spirit*. Who is the Spirit? We have to admit that the Spirit must be the Holy Spirit. Therefore, the Son is called the Father, and the Son, who is the very Lord, is also the Spirit. This means the Father, Son, and Spirit are One. We emphasize this matter because it is by His different Persons that God works out His economy. Without these different Persons—the Person of the Father, the Person of the Son, and the Person of the Spirit—God could never bring Himself into us.

Matthew 28:19 says: "Go ye therefore, and make disciples...baptizing them into the name of the Father and of the Son and of the Holy Spirit." It does not say, baptizing them into the name of any one divine Person. Nor does it say "in the names," but in "the name (singular) of the Father and of the Son and of the Holy Spirit." Why do we need to be baptized into the name of the Father and of the Son and of the Spirit? Furthermore, if we check the original Greek, we will discover that the preposition "in," used in the King James Version, is the preposition "into" or "unto" (eis). Hence, it reads, "baptized into the name," not "in the name." The same word is used in Romans 6:3, "...baptized into Christ," which is the proper translation. What does all this mean?

Let me illustrate it in this way: if you buy a watermelon, your intention is to eat and digest this melon. In other words, your intention is to work this melon into you. How can this be done? First, you buy the whole melon; second, you cut it into slices; then, thirdly, before this melon enters your stomach, you chew it until it becomes juice. The sequence is: melon, slices, and finally juice. Are these three different things or just one? I believe this is the best illustration of the Trinity. Most melons are larger than your stomach. How can you swallow a large melon when your mouth is so small and your throat is so slender? Before it can become the proper size for you to eat, it must be cut into slices. Then, once it is eaten, it becomes juice. Are the slices not the melon? And is the juice not the melon? If we say that they are not, we must be most ignorant.

The Father is illustrated by the whole melon; the Son by the slices; and finally, the Spirit by the juice. Now you see the point: The Father is not only the Father, but is also the Son. And the Son is not only the Son, but is also the Spirit. In other words, this melon is also the slices to eat and the juice within us. The melon disappears after it is eaten. Originally, the melon was on the table, but after being eaten, the melon is *in* the whole family.

In the Gospel of John the Father is in the first chapters; the Son as the expression of the Father, is in the succeeding chapters; and eventually, the Spirit, as the Breath of the Son, is in chapter 20 (verse 22). This one Gospel reveals the Father, the Son, and the Spirit. Read the whole twenty-one chapters in this book. First, it says: "In the beginning was the Word, and the Word was with God, and the Word was God...And the Word became flesh, and dwelt among us." This very Word, which is God Himself, one day became a man and dwelt among us—not within us but among us. Then He lived on the earth for thirty-three and a half years. He eventually died and was raised again. This is mysterious, miraculous, wonderful; we can never fathom it. The night after His resurrection, He came to His disciples in His resurrected body. All the doors were shut, yet He entered in bodily and showed to the disciples His hands and His side. We cannot comprehend this. He came in a very miraculous and mysterious way. Finally, He breathed on the disciples and told them to receive the Holy Spirit. That very breath is the Holy Spirit, like the juice of the melon.

From that time, I would ask you, where is Jesus in the Gospel of John? After He came to the disciples, this Gospel never mentions the ascension of Jesus to the heavens. Then where is this Wonderful One at the end of this Gospel? Like the watermelon in the stomach, He is within the disciples through the Spirit as the breath.

God's economy is to work Himself into us by means of His three Persons. There is need of the three Persons of the

Godhead, for without these three Persons, God could never be wrought into us. It is just like the illustration of the melon. Without being cut into slices and received as juice, the watermelon could never be wrought into us. God could be wrought into us *only* by His three different Persons.

THE MIND, THE HEART, AND THE IMAGE

Let us now turn to ourselves and consider what we are as containers. Do not think that we are so simple. I believe the medical doctors could tell us that the human body is very delicate and complicated. A human being is not a simple container, like a bottle containing a beverage; on the contrary, man has many different parts. This is why we must know the different parts of man as well as the three Persons of God in order to hit the mark of God's economy. God's economy involves His three Persons, and the mark of His economy involves our different parts.

So many of us drive a car. But it is impossible to drive a car unless we know some of its parts. We must learn at least the essential parts for its operation. For example, we need to identify and locate such parts as the brake, the gear shift, the ignition, etc. If we do not know the parts of the car, we do not know how to operate it. Likewise, in order for us to realize how we can contain God, we must know the different parts of our being.

Consider how many parts are found in a short passage in 2 Corinthians 4. In verse four there is the *mind,* and in verse six the *heart.* At least two parts, the mind and the heart, are found in this passage. Perhaps you have been a Christian for many years, and up to this very time you do not know the difference between the mind and the heart. We read that the mind could be blinded by the enemy and the heart could be enlightened by the light of God. The god of this age blinds the minds of the unbelievers, but God shines His light into the hearts of the believers. Perhaps you thought that you understood this part of the Word, but never considered that here are two parts of the human being.

Before defining the mind and the heart from the Scriptures, let us use the camera as an illustration. The camera was made to take something in. To take a picture means to take something into the camera. When I visited Tokyo, I used my camera to take Tokyo in. My intention was that an image *outside* the camera should be brought *inside* the camera.

What was necessary for me to take a picture into the camera? Three main things: the lens without, the film within, and the light. With these three things, an object can be taken into the camera. Several years ago when I was traveling on the train, I took some pictures. After the films were processed, many of them were blank. What had happened? I discovered that I was in such a hurry to take the pictures that I forgot to take the cover off the lens. The lens was blinded by the covering.

Many times, when an unbeliever comes to hear a good message of the Gospel, we think, "Oh, tonight this man will surely be saved!" But eventually, he is still blank. The enemy of God has blinded his mind. The mind is the understanding organ, and Satan has blinded the understanding of this listener. Regardless how good the message is and how much he has heard, yet his understanding has been blinded, or covered. His mind is still a blank, nothing has been taken in.

Thirty years ago Brother Watchman Nee was preaching the Gospel, telling people that God's intention was not for us to do good. Good does not mean anything to God. He stressed this point so much that it was very clear. A brother had brought a friend to the meeting, and, looking at his friend from time to time during the message, he noticed that he was always nodding his head positively as if he understood. The brother was so happy, thinking his friend was listening carefully and taking everything in. Do you know what happened? Afterwards, the brother asked his friend, "What do you think about the message?" He replied, "Yes, all religions encourage people to do good!" But in his message Brother Nee had stressed so clearly that God had no intention to require man to do good. This man's reply indicated that his understanding was blinded by the enemy. Many times we need to pray that God would bind the god of this age, bind his blinding work during a message. This simply means to take the cover off the lens.

After the cover is taken off, we need the right kind of film. Without the proper film, even though the lens is right, it will not work. We cannot receive a proper picture if we are using the wrong film. The film illustrates our heart. Our mind is like the lens, and our heart is like the film. Therefore, our heart must be tuned and adjusted properly. We need the lens, and we also need the film. We need the understanding mind, and we need the receiving heart. The heart must be pure, clean, right, adjusted.

Yet, even if we have the lens and the film, we still need the light. We need the light to shine through the lens and onto the film. The divine light of God's glory shines upon us to give the image and picture of Christ. This very image of Christ is the treasure in the earthen vessels. Through this illustration we can realize how to deal with our mind and our heart. It is just like the camera: we must know how to adjust the lens and how to use the film. If we do not know how to handle the lens and the film, we can never receive a proper picture.

Spiritual experiences are just like taking pictures. We ourselves are the cameras, and we must learn how to use our camera in order to receive God in Christ as the picture. It is regrettable that so many dear Christians simply do not know how to handle their minds and their hearts. In fact, they do not even know that they themselves are cameras.

Christianity is not, strictly speaking, a religion teaching people to do this and to do that. It is simply Christ Himself, the living One, being wrought into us. He is the very object, the very figure, and we are the camera. As the object, He must be wrought into us by the shining of the divine light through the lens onto the film. Day by day and moment by moment, we need the divine light to shine more of the image of Christ through the understanding of the mind that we may receive Him into our heart. Therefore, we must learn how to adjust the mind and the heart.

What are the spiritual experiences? They are simply the pictures of Christ taken into us, the camera, and impressed upon our spiritual film. With some Christians the lens is nearly always covered, and the film is usually improperly adjusted. If you look at their film there is no picture; every photo of the film is blank, because there are no experiences of Christ. But if the Apostle Paul came and we opened his camera and took out the film, we would find that every photo is a picture full of Christ. Everything depends on how much we adjust the lens and take care of the film—i.e., how much we deal with our mind and properly tune our heart. If we do this well, whenever the divine light shines upon us, the *image of Christ* will be shined into us. We will have a beautiful picture of Christ. This is God's economy with its mark.

Now we know the importance of learning our different parts. We were made to contain God in every part. We must go on to know them all—more than even the mind and heart. In the next chapter we will consider in detail all the parts, and later, how they function and how to adjust them.

CHAPTER SIX

THE INWARD AND THE HIDDEN PARTS

Let us now go on to see the details of the vessel of the Lord. In the previous chapter we have seen that we were created purposely to be His containers, having God Himself as our content. For this purpose God has created us with many "parts." Do not think that the term "parts" originated with me. God says, in Jeremiah 31:33, "I will put my law in their *inward parts.*" The inward parts are within our soul; they are not the outward members of our body. God also says that He will write His laws in our *heart*. What, then, are the inward parts, and what is the heart?

If we compare Jeremiah 31:33 with the quotation in Hebrews 8:10, "I will put my laws into their mind," we will see a slight, but important variation. Jeremiah says "into their inward parts," but Hebrews renders it, "into their mind." This comparison proves that the mind is one of the inward parts.

The term "inward parts" is used in the Scriptures more than once. For example, Psalm 51:6: "Behold, thou desirest truth in the inward parts." The inward parts must have truth. Besides the inward parts, there is another part in this Psalm called "the hidden part": "And in the hidden part thou wilt make me to know wisdom." The truth is in the inward parts, but wisdom is in the hidden part. We need to find out what are these inward parts, and what is the hidden part.

THE THREE PARTS OF MAN—SPIRIT, SOUL, BODY

Some passages to which we will refer are very familiar. First Thessalonians 5:23 is a verse indicating that we are tripartite, or, of three parts: the spirit, the soul, and the body. We can illustrate this by three concentric circles:

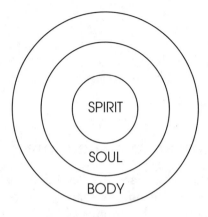

Hebrews 4:12 also mentions the spirit and the soul, and the dividing of these two parts. If we would know Christ and enter into Him as the good land and as the rest, we must discern the spirit from the soul. The spirit is the very place where Christ dwells in us; so if we would know Christ in an experiential way, we must discern our human spirit from our soul. This verse mentions the difference not only between the spirit and the soul, but also between the joints and the marrow of the body and between the thoughts and the intents of the heart. The living Word of God is a discerner of all these things. This proves that if we are going to know the Lord in a practical and real way, we must discern all these parts. What are the thoughts of the heart and the intents of the heart? And how many parts are in the heart?

In Luke 1:46-47, the soul and the spirit are again distinguished.

Philippians 1:27 says that we must be of one spirit—not the Holy Spirit, but the human spirit—and of one soul. (In the King James Version "one soul" is rendered "one mind.") Again, this verse shows that there is a difference between the spirit and the soul.

Finally, Mark 12:30 says, "And thou shalt love the Lord thy God with all thy heart, and with all thy soul, and with all thy mind, and with all thy strength." Here are four different parts: the heart, the soul, the mind, and the strength. If we put all these verses together we will realize that there are quite a number of different parts within us besides the many parts of the body.

First Thessalonians 5:23 indicates that we are spirit, soul and body, and Psalm 51 reveals the inward parts with the hidden part. The inward parts are the parts of the soul, which is proved by comparing Hebrews 8:10 with Jeremiah 31:33, where "the mind" is quoted as a variation of "the inward parts." Just as the inward parts must be the parts of the soul, so the hidden part must be the spirit. Of all our parts, the spirit is the most hidden one within us. This inmost part is not only hidden within the body, but is even hidden within the soul. Hence, there are the *outward* parts of the body, the *inward* parts of the soul, and the *hidden* part of the spirit.

THE THREE PARTS OF THE SOUL— MIND, WILL, EMOTION

There are three parts to the soul and three parts to the spirit. We must discover what are the three parts of both the soul and the spirit. Furthermore, we must also define the heart. First Thessalonians 5:23 indicates that we are a tripartite being—spirit, soul, and body—but it does not mention the heart. What is the heart and how can we relate it with the inward parts and the hidden part?

God's Word proves clearly and definitely that the soul is of three parts—the mind, the will, and the emotion. The shaded area in the diagram below illustrates the parts of the soul.

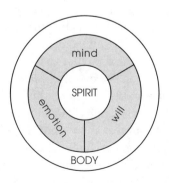

Proverbs 2:10 suggests that the soul needs *knowledge.*
Note also Proverbs 19:2 and 24:14. Since knowledge is a function of the mind, this proves that the mind is a part of the
soul. All three of these verses from Proverbs tell us that we
need to have knowledge in the soul. Then Psalm 139:14 says
the soul *knows.* To know is something of the mind, which
again proves that the mind is a part of the soul. Psalm 13:2
says the soul *considers,* or *counsels,* which refers to the mind.
Lamentations 3:20 indicates that *remembrance* is of the soul.
That is, the soul can remember things. From these verses we
can see that there is a part in the soul that knows, considers,
and remembers. This part is called the mind.

The second part of the soul is the will. Job 7:15 says
the soul *chooses.* To choose something is a decision made
by the act of the will. This proves that the will must be a part
of the soul. Job 6:7 says the soul *refuses.* To choose and refuse
are both functions of the will. First Chronicles 22:19 says,
"set your soul to *seek.*" Just as we set our minds to think, so
we set our souls to seek. This is, of course, the soul making a
decision, which proves that the will must be a part of the soul.
Then in Numbers 30, *"bind his soul"* is mentioned ten times.
When we read this chapter, we understand that to bind the
soul is to make a decision. It deals with a vow that is made
with the Lord. To make a decision to bind the soul is to make
a vow to the Lord. Thus, it is proven that the will must be a
part of the soul. Psalm 27:12, 41:2, and Ezekiel 16:27 translate the Hebrew word "soul" into *"will."* The prayer made by
the Psalmist is, "Do not deliver me to the will of the enemy."
In the original it means, "Do not deliver me to the soul of the
enemy." This proves clearly that the will must be a part of the
soul.

The emotion is the third part of the soul. With the emotion
there are many aspects: for example, love, hatred, joy, grief,
etc. All of these are expressions of the emotion. References
to *love* are found in 1 Samuel 18:1, Song of Solomon 1:7, and
Psalm 42:1. These verses show that love is something in
the soul, proving, therefore, that within the soul there is such
an organ or function as the emotion. Concerning *hatred,*
note 2 Samuel 5:8, Psalm 107:18, and Ezekiel 36:5. These

passages indicate that hatred is something of the soul. Since hatred is an expression of the emotion, these verses also prove that the emotion must be a part of the soul. Ezekiel 36:5 is better translated in the American Standard Version, where the term "despite of soul" is used. It means the dislike or hatred of the soul. *Joy,* an element of the emotion, is also a part of the soul, as seen in Isaiah 61:10 and Psalm 86:4, again proving that emotion is a part of the soul. Then there is the matter of *grief,* mentioned in 1 Samuel 30:6 and Judges 10:16. Grief is another expression of the soul. Another aspect is *desire:* 1 Samuel 20:4, Deuteronomy 14:26, Ezekiel 24:25, and Jeremiah 44:14. As to Ezekiel 24:25 and Jeremiah 44:14, the right meaning is reached when the American Standard Version is checked with the Young's or Strong's Concordance. Desire, an element of the emotion, is shown by these verses to be in the realm of the soul.

These verses establish the ground to verify the three parts in the soul: the mind, the will, and the emotion. In the Scriptures it is difficult to find any additional parts of the soul, for these three parts cover all the functions of the soul. The mind is the leading part, followed by the will and the emotion. These are the verses which best reveal what are the three parts of the soul.

THE THREE PARTS OF THE SPIRIT—CONSCIENCE, FELLOWSHIP, INTUITION

It is interesting to note that there are three Persons of the Godhead, three parts of man's being, three inward parts of the soul, and also three parts to the spirit. All are in *three* parts. The Scriptures also reveal three parts in the tabernacle, the building of God. Three is the basic figure or number. Even in Noah's ark there are three levels. With the tabernacle the number three is used many times. For example, the width of one board is one and a half cubits. When two boards are joined as a pair, the total width is three cubits. This means that the number three is a whole unit.

Therefore, the spirit is a complete unit, composed of three parts or functions: conscience, fellowship, and intuition. The shaded area in the diagram below illustrates the parts of the spirit.

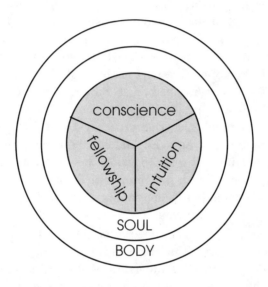

It is easy to understand the *conscience*. We are all familiar with this. To perceive right from wrong is one function of the conscience. To condemn or to justify is another one of its functions. It is also easy to comprehend the *fellowship*. The fellowship is our communion with God. Within our spirit, such a function makes it possible to contact God. In a simple word, fellowship is to touch God. But it is not very easy to understand the intuition. Intuition means to have a direct sense or knowledge. There is such a direct sense in our spirit, regardless of reason, circumstances, or background. It is a sense without reason, a sense that is not "reasonable." It is a direct sense of God and a direct knowledge from God. This function is what we call the intuition of the spirit. Thus, the spirit is known by the functions of the conscience, the fellowship, and the intuition.

But these three parts in the human spirit must be proven from the Scriptures. First of all, the conscience is found in

Romans 9:1, "My conscience bearing witness with me in the Holy Spirit." Comparing Romans 9:1 with Romans 8:16, the conscience is located in the human spirit. On one hand, the Holy Spirit bears witness with our spirit. On the other hand, our conscience bears witness with the Holy Spirit. This proves that the conscience must be a function of our spirit. In 1 Corinthians 5:3, the Apostle Paul says that in his spirit he judged a sinful person. To judge means either to condemn or to justify, which are acts of the conscience. But the Apostle says, in my *spirit* I judge. This confirms that the condemning or justifying function is in the spirit; hence, the conscience is in the spirit. Psalm 51:10 speaks of "a right spirit within me"—that is, a spirit which is right. Knowing right from wrong is related to the conscience, so this verse also proves that the conscience is in the spirit. Psalm 34:18 refers to "a contrite spirit." To be contrite means we realize we are wrong. In other words, we accuse and condemn ourselves, which is a function of the conscience. "A contrite spirit" shows that the conscience is related to the spirit. Deuteronomy 2:30 says, "hardened his spirit," which means that the conscience was hardened. To be hardened in the spirit means to be careless with the conscience. When we cast off the feeling in the conscience, we become hardened in the spirit. These verses offer the strongest ground for the fact that the function of the conscience is in the human spirit.

Let us go on to find the Scriptural ground for the fellowship. First of all, John 4:24 tells us that we must worship God in our spirit. To worship God requires worship in our spirit. To worship God is to contact God and fellowship with God. This verse proves that the function of worship or of fellowship is in our spirit. In Romans 1:9 the Apostle Paul says, "I serve God with my spirit." To serve God is also a type of fellowship with God. So this also proves that the organ for fellowship is in our spirit. Romans 7:6 must be added: "we serve in newness of the spirit." In other words, service is essentially fellowship with the Lord in our spirit.

Let us consider Ephesians 6:18. The Greek interlinear text translates this verse as, "praying always in spirit..." There is no article before "spirit," neither is it capitalized. It does not mean the Holy Spirit, but our human spirit. To pray means to fellowship with God. To pray in spirit indicates, then, that fellowship with God is a matter in our spirit. Luke 1:47 says, "My spirit hath rejoiced in God." This means that the human spirit has contacted God. Once again, fellowship with God is a function in the spirit. Then, Romans 8:16: "the Spirit bears witness with our spirit." This verse is very clear, because it shows that fellowship with God must be both in our spirit and in the Spirit of God. First Corinthians 6:17: "He that is joined unto the Lord is one spirit." Real fellowship means that we become one spirit with the Lord. This fellowship is in the spirit. All of these verses are sufficient to prove that the function of fellowship is in our human spirit.

How about the intuition? Although it is difficult to find the Scriptural ground for this function, there are some verses. First Corinthians 2:11 reveals that the spirit of man can know what the soul cannot. Our spirit can discern that which the soul cannot discern. This proves that something extra is in our spirit. Our soul can know things by reason and by circumstantial experiences, but the human spirit can discern things without these. This direct sense shows that the intuition is in our spirit. Then there is Mark 2:8, which says, "perceiving in his spirit." Mark 8:12 says, "sighed deeply in his spirit." John 11:33: "groaned in the spirit." To perceive, to sigh, and to groan in our spirit come from a direct sense of discernment which is not dependent upon reason. This we call the intuition, the third function of our spirit.

Now we have the Scriptural ground for these six parts: the three parts of the soul and the three parts of the spirit.

THE FOUR PARTS OF THE HEART—MIND, WILL, EMOTION, CONSCIENCE

What, then, is the heart? The heart is not a separate part in addition to the soul and the spirit, but a composition of all the parts of the soul and the first part of the spirit. It includes the mind, the will, and the emotion plus one part of the spirit, the conscience. The shaded area in the following diagram illustrates the parts composing the heart.

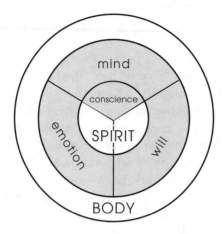

Man does not have more than three main parts in his whole being. As a human being we have a body, soul, and spirit. We do not have a fourth and separate part such as the heart.

Now we need to confirm that the mind, the first part of the soul, is a part of the heart. Matthew 9:4 says, "Think ye...in your hearts?" Therefore, in the heart one can think. Since the thinking processes are in the mind, this proves that the mind is a part of the heart. Genesis 6:5: "the thoughts of his heart." The thoughts are something of the mind, but Genesis 6:5 mentions the thoughts of the heart. The same is seen in Hebrews 4:12: "the thoughts...of the heart." These three passages are ample proof that the mind, an organ of the soul, is a part of the heart.

The will is seen in Acts 11:23: "purpose of heart," or "purpose in the heart." Purpose is a function of the will, but in Acts it is something of the heart. This shows that the will is also a part of the heart. Hebrews 4:12 speaks of the "intents of the heart." The intents correspond to the purposes, which are of the will. Again, this proves that the will is a part of the heart. There are more verses, but these two are enough. To quote the Scriptural standard, only two witnesses are required.

The emotion is found in John 16:22: "your heart shall rejoice." To rejoice is an element of the emotions, but here the Lord says that the heart rejoices. Therefore, this confirms that the emotion is also a part of the heart. In the same chapter the Lord says, "sorrow has filled your hearts" (v. 6). Sorrow is also something of emotion. So these two verses verify that the emotion is also a part in the heart.

Concerning the conscience, Hebrews 10:22 says, "our hearts sprinkled from an evil conscience." So we see that the conscience has much to do with the heart. If we are going to have a pure heart, we must have a conscience that is without offense. Our conscience has to be sprinkled in order to have a pure heart. Thus, without a doubt, the conscience is a part of the heart. First John 3:20 mentions that "our heart condemns." To condemn is the function of the conscience. So this verse proves that the conscience is also a part of the heart.

Scriptural ground has thus been given to prove that all the parts of the soul and the first part of the spirit—the four parts of the mind, the will, the emotion and the conscience—composed together equal the heart.

CHAPTER SEVEN

THE FUNCTION OF THE INWARD AND THE HIDDEN PARTS

We must continue to see the inward parts and the hidden part of our being. We must remember these two terms, the inward parts and the hidden part. The inward parts of our being are the parts of the soul, and the hidden part is our spirit. With both our soul and our spirit there are three parts, while the heart is composed of the three parts of the soul combined with the first part of the spirit. We must spend time to consider the details of all these parts. We must first see what is the function of the heart and how to deal with it. Then we must see the spirit, and finally, the soul. Let us look to the Lord that we may have grace to see all these parts clearly, that we may be sufficiently impressed to learn all the parts of our being, and that we may know how to exercise our spirit and our heart in order to experience the Lord. In this chapter we must see the functions of the heart, the spirit, and the soul.

According to the record of the Scriptures, the heart has to be dealt with first, not the spirit or the soul. The reason for this is that the heart is a composition of all the parts of the soul and the most important part of the spirit, the conscience. Our relationship with the Lord must start with the conscience. If our conscience is wrong, we can be sure that we are wrong both with God and with others. Therefore, since the conscience is the main part of the heart, the heart must be dealt with first to insure a proper relationship with God.

THE HEART AS THE LOVING ORGAN

Second Corinthians 3:16 says, "Nevertheless when it (the heart) turns to the Lord, the veil shall be taken away." The

heart must first be turned to the Lord. This is real repentance. When we were fallen, our heart was turned *away from*
the Lord. But when we repented, our heart was turned *to* the
Lord. This matter of turning the heart to the Lord is not done
once for all. The heart must be turned to the Lord all the
time, day by day. Every morning we must turn our heart
again toward the Lord. After rising, we should go to the Lord
and tell Him, "Lord, here I am. By Thy mercy and grace I
wish to turn my heart anew to Thee for this day."

When our heart is turned to the Lord, the veil is gone. So
many people say, "Oh, why don't I have guidance? Why don't
I know the Lord's will?" But the problem is, where is their
heart and in what direction is their heart? Their heart must
be turned and tuned to the Lord. When I was young, I used to

pray over 2 Corinthians 3:16 nearly every day, "Lord, cause
me to turn my heart to Thee." Oh, it works! Just try it. Before
you read the Word in the morning, first of all, turn your heart
to the Lord. The veil will be gone and there will be light. The
veil which is between you and the Lord will be taken away by
turning your heart to Him, and you will see the light.

Once our heart is turned to the Lord, it must next exercise
faith. Romans 10:9-10 says: "believe in thy heart," and "with
the heart man believeth." To believe is not an exercise of
the spirit, the mind, or the will, but an exercise of the heart:
"for with the heart man believeth." We need to learn how to
exercise our heart to believe in order to cooperate with the
indwelling Spirit. After our heart is turned to the Lord, we
should immediately exercise faith in our heart. Whatever
the Lord says in the Word, we must exercise our heart to
believe. Whatever we sense deeply within, we must believe by
exercising the heart. We must believe in the Lord in the midst
of our environment. In all the situations within our set of circumstances, we must always exercise our heart to believe the
Lord. To exercise faith in the Lord will keep the heart from
doubt. We must even pray that the Lord will protect our heart
from doubt.

Thirdly, the heart must be sprinkled from an evil conscience (Heb. 10:22). The heart itself is not to be sprinkled,
but the evil conscience. Our conscience always needs the

sprinkling of the redeeming blood of the Lord Jesus. The more we turn our heart to the Lord and the more we believe in the Lord by exercising our heart, the more we will feel in our conscience that we are wrong in many matters. When our heart is not turned to the Lord, we will never sense that our conscience is wrong. When our heart is turned away from the Lord we have only one sense: that we are right in everything; everyone else is wrong, but we ourselves are right. When we turn our heart to the Lord, we can only see ourselves; we cannot see others. The more we believe in Him, the more we will sense how wrong we are in so many things. We are wrong with our wife, with our husband, with our children, with our parents, with our schoolmates. What are these accusations in our heart? They are the accusations of our conscience. At this time we will spontaneously confess everything according to the inner accusation of our conscience. The more we confess, the more the blood of the Lord Jesus will be applied to our conscience. It will be purged, cleansed, and without offense—a pure conscience. To have our heart sprinkled from an evil conscience means that our conscience has been so purged that there is no more condemnation in our heart. Our heart is at peace and full of joy in the Lord.

Furthermore, according to Ezekiel 36:26, the heart must be renewed. In Ezekiel 36:25, the Lord said, "I will sprinkle clean water upon you, and ye shall be clean from all your filthiness, and from all your idols will I cleanse you." But this is not all. To cleanse us from all filthiness, from all sins, and even from idols is only on the negative side. We need something positive. Therefore, in the next verse it says, "a new heart also will I give you." A new heart is the old heart renewed.

Thus, there are four steps in dealing with the heart. They do not take place once for all when we believe in the Lord Jesus and receive Him as our Savior. We who are seeking the Lord must have our heart refreshed by these four steps every day. We must turn our heart to the Lord, exercise our heart to believe Him, have our heart sprinkled from an evil conscience, and have it renewed again and again. The renewing of the heart is not a once for all matter. I believe that the

Apostle Paul, if he were living today, would still need to have his heart renewed. We must put all these steps into practice immediately. When we first rise up in the morning, we must pray, "Lord, cause me to turn my heart to You." Then we need to exercise our heart to believe the Lord: "Lord, I believe You and Your Word. I believe in Your dealing within me and in all Your dealings in my environment." At this point we will sense how wrong we are, how many mistakes we have made, and how much filthiness we have. Therefore, we must confess in order to be cleansed and sprinkled from an evil conscience. Then our heart will be renewed afresh.

These four steps will cause the heart to function adequately. The function of the heart is to love the Lord, for it is the loving organ of our being. This is proven by Mark 12:30: "Thou shalt love the Lord with all thy heart." The heart was created for the purpose of loving the Lord. If we do not have a heart, we cannot love. Could we see without eyes? Could we hear without ears? Could we think without a mind? No! Neither could we love without the heart. Many Christians do not know what is the function of the heart. They know the function of the eyes, the ears, and the mind, but they simply do not know the function of the heart.

Love is a matter of the heart. People cannot be loved with our nose; nor can they be loved with our hands. The heart is the only organ to exercise love. No one can say that they do not love anything. Everyone loves something—either the Lord Himself or something else. The more we turn our heart to the Lord, the more we will exercise our heart to believe the Lord, and the more our heart will be sprinkled from an evil conscience and renewed. Then it will have a greater capacity to love the Lord. This is the function of a renewed heart. Every morning we must renew our heart so that we may love the Lord more and more.

All spiritual experiences start with love in the heart. If we do not love the Lord, it is impossible to receive any kind of spiritual experience. In fact, the first experience of our Christian life, salvation, involves the heart loving the Lord Jesus. Not one person who really repents is without love in his heart toward the Lord. Perhaps they do not have the language to express it, but they have the sweet sense of love within. They do not have the knowledge, but their initial *experience* of salvation is a reaction or reflection of love in their heart to the Lord.

We all must learn how to continually turn and exercise our heart, to have our heart purged from an evil conscience and renewed again so that we may love the Lord more and more. It was the loss of its first, fresh love to the Lord that was the cause of the Church's fall and degradation. When our heart is not fresh in loving the Lord, we have fallen. We must turn our heart back to the Lord again and again and have it continually renewed that we may have a new and fresh love toward the Lord.

THE SPIRIT AS THE RECEIVING ORGAN

Now that we have seen the function of the heart, we need to consider the function of the spirit. First of all, the Bible tells us that we were originally dead, but when we received the Lord Jesus, we were quickened and made alive. What does it mean that we were dead? When I was young, I could not understand. I said to myself, "How can they say that I am dead when I am still alive?" Later on, of course, I learned that I was dead in my spirit. It was my spirit that was dead and out of function. The function of the spirit is to contact God, commune with God, and receive and worship God. But due to the fall, the spirit became dormant and could not function.

When we received the Lord Jesus as our Savior, the Holy Spirit—and we must remind ourselves that when the title "Holy Spirit" is used, it means the all-inclusive Spirit—came into our spirit and touched our spirit. By such a touch, our spirit was quickened. The word quickened cannot be adequately translated in our language. In Greek, it means something like this: "just by touching, life is ministered and imparted."

Perhaps this could be illustrated by electricity: when we touch electricity, something of electricity is transmitted into us. By a simple, little touch electricity is transmitted. Similarly, the Holy Spirit came into our spirit to touch our spirit, and by that touch, the very life which is the Lord Himself was imparted into us. Our dead, dormant spirit immediately became alive. This is something more than a miracle. Many times we have thought that it would be wonderful and miraculous if a dead person were resurrected. But we must realize that when the Holy Spirit quickens our dead spirit, it is even more miraculous. History records that thousands and even millions of people have been rapidly changed, because their dead spirit became alive. In just one second a person dead in the spirit can be made alive. The Holy Spirit is much more powerful than electricity and much faster than its transmission.

Colossians 2:13 and Ephesians 2:1, 5 say that the spirit was dead and then quickened. We were dead in sins and then quickened with Christ. These two passages prove that we were originally dead in the spirit, but when we received the Lord Jesus as our Savior, our dead spirit was quickened and made alive. When our spirit was made alive, it was also regenerated. The prefix "re-" of regeneration means "again." This means that our spirit was not only made alive, but also that another life was added into our spirit. This other life is the divine and uncreated life of God. It is Christ Himself. When the Holy Spirit, based upon the redeeming work of Christ, came into us, He not only quickened our dead spirit but also brought Christ into our spirit. This new life added into our spirit is something more than God gave us at creation.

Therefore, not only has our dead spirit been recovered and made alive, but a new substance has been added into our spirit. This additional new substance or essence is Christ Himself. This is the new birth, the regeneration. John 3:6 says, "that which is born of the Spirit is spirit." By the new birth, or regeneration, something other than what we originally had was added to us. We must say this again and again: something has been added. Not only has the old and the dead been renewed and quickened, but Christ Himself has been added into us as the very essence of divine life. This is regeneration and the new life. By all this we now have a new spirit (Ezek. 36:26).

May I ask: Have you received Christ Himself as your new life? If you answer "yes," I would ask: Then why are you still so poor? Christians need to know this Christ as a living reality. Atomic power is not only something outward, but something inward. Even within a mere piece of paper, there is atomic power. But when you received Christ, something more powerful than atomic power was added into your spirit. If you believe this, you have to jump up and say, "Hallelujah!" You have to thank and praise Him that such a wonderful, all-inclusive, exhaustless, immeasurable Christ has actually been added into you. We simply do not have adequate words to describe the Christ who has come into us. Only eternity can tell the story.

But, praise Him, this is not all. Our spirit is also *indwelt by the all-inclusive Holy Spirit.* When we were saved, God not only renewed our heart and our spirit, but He also put His own Spirit into us (Ezek. 36:26, 27; John 14:17). This wonderful Spirit dwells (Rom. 8:11) in our human spirit (Rom. 8:16). Our spirit is the very residence of the Holy Spirit. Consider how wonderful this Spirit is. From the time of our salvation, our dead spirit has become a spirit that is quickened, regenerated with Christ as the divine life, and indwelt by the all-inclusive Holy Spirit. We *now* have such a spirit.

But even this is not all. Our spirit is now joined to the Lord *as one spirit.* Our spirit and the Lord Himself as the Spirit are joined together as one spirit (1 Cor. 6:17). No human words can exhaust this mystery.

What is the purpose and function of the spirit? It is to contact the Lord, to receive Him, to worship God (John 4:24), and to fellowship with the divine Persons of the Triune God. The heart is the loving organ, whereas the spirit is the contacting and receiving organ. We cannot love with our spirit. We must love with our heart. But the One whom our heart loves must be contacted and received by our spirit.

I will never forget a sister who was bothered by this kind of message. She thought that if our heart loved the Lord, it was good enough, and there was no need to talk about the spirit. She thought the spirit and the heart were synonymous terms. Probably after hearing this kind of message, this sister had not slept well that night, for the next morning while at breakfast, she asked, "Isn't it enough that our hearts love the Lord? Why is there a need for us to talk about the spirit?" I replied, "Sister, here I have a nice Bible. Do you love it?" She answered, "Of course, I love it." Then I said, "Take it!" When she stretched out her hand, I said, "Don't! Don't exercise your hand! It is your heart that loves the Bible. As long as your heart loves the Bible, that is all right. There is no need to exercise your hand to take it." The point is clear. We cannot say that as long as the heart loves the Lord, it is good enough. The spirit is necessary to take Christ.

Suppose I love my breakfast. As long as my heart loves bacon, toast, milk, juice, etc., is that enough? Absolutely not! If this is enough, I am afraid that after some days I will be buried. To love is a matter of the heart; but in order to receive something, another organ must be exercised. The organ we need to exercise depends upon what we are going to receive. If we are going to receive food, of course, we have to exercise the mouth; if we are going to receive a voice, we have to exercise our ears. If we are going to receive colorful scenery, we must exercise our eyes. Now, since we love the Lord, what organ must we exercise in order to receive Him? The eyes? The more we look for Him, the more the Lord will disappear. God purposely created only one organ to receive and contact Him. That is the spirit. The spirit within us has the same function spiritually as the stomach has physically. It was specifically created for the purpose of receiving God into us.

But before we can receive something, we must have a love for it. No one receives anything if he does not love it first. If you do not love your breakfast, it is rather hard for you to receive it. This is why you must first have an appetite. When we love the Lord, we will then take Him, contact Him, commune with Him, and fellowship with Him. The heart is for us to love, but the spirit is for us to receive. By the renewing of the heart, we have a new interest and a new desire to love the Lord. By the renewing of the spirit, we have a new ability and a new capacity to receive the Lord. Therefore, after our spirit has been quickened and Christ as life has been added to it, after it has been indwelt by the Holy Spirit and joined with the Lord as one spirit, it then becomes a very keen organ to receive and contact the Lord.

THE SOUL AS THE REFLECTING ORGAN

Next, we must deal with the soul. The first thing we must learn in dealing with the soul is to deny it. Two passages, Matthew 16:24-26 and Luke 9:23-25, tell us clearly that we need to deny our soul, which is the self. In the previous chapter, we have seen that the soul, our very self, is composed of three parts: the mind, the will, and the emotion. Therefore, we must learn to deny our natural mind, our natural will, and our natural emotion.

Secondly, the soul must be purified (1 Pet. 1:22), which is accomplished mainly by receiving the Word. The Word of God can purify the soul from so many fleshly, worldly, and natural things. Our soul is our self, our very being, which has been extensively damaged and occupied by carnal, worldly, and natural things. Therefore, we must first deny our soul; then, the more we deny our soul, the more it will be purified by the Word of God.

Thirdly, our soul must be transformed (2 Cor. 3:18 and Rom. 12:2). Second Corinthians 3:18 says that we must be transformed, but it does not indicate in what part we are to be transformed. However, Romans 12:2 shows that we are transformed by the renewing of the mind. Transformation, therefore, is to be accomplished in our soul, because the mind is the leading part of the soul. After our spirit has been regenerated, our soul needs to be transformed.

The soul has to be denied, then purified, then transformed into the image of Christ—but for what purpose? We have pointed out that the purpose of the heart is to love the Lord, and the purpose of the spirit is to receive and contact the Lord. But what is the purpose of the soul? It is to *reflect* the Lord. In most versions the word "reflecting" is not translated in 2 Corinthians 3:18, but the meaning is in the original language. "Reflecting" is the function of a mirror, which with open face beholds and reflects. The soul, by being purified and transformed, becomes the very organ, as a mirror, to reflect and express Christ. Thus, we love Him with our *heart,* we receive and contact Him with our *spirit,* and we reflect and express Him with our transformed *soul.* We must put all these things into practice in our daily life. Then our lives will verify that what has been explained here is entirely practical and really works.

CHAPTER EIGHT

DEALING WITH THE HEART
AND THE SPIRIT

We have seen the definition and function of the heart, the spirit and the soul. Our relationship with the Lord is always begun and maintained by the heart. Of course, to contact the Lord is a matter of the spirit, but this must be initiated and maintained by the heart, for our heart is the gateway of our whole being. A building with many rooms always has an entrance and an exit; a person comes in by the entrance and goes out by the exit. When the entrance is closed, everyone is kept away from the rooms inside the building, but once it has been opened, people can enter the building and enjoy each room.

The heart is not a separate and exclusive part of our being, but is composed of all the parts of the soul and a part of the spirit. Therefore, being such a composition, the heart becomes the very gateway of our whole being. In other words, the heart becomes both the entrance and the exit of our being. Whatever enters into us must enter through the heart. Whatever comes out from us must proceed through the heart.

For example, if our heart is not alert as we listen to a message, we will not get the substance of it. Or, when we are reading, we will receive nothing if our heart is not upon the content. Even while eating, if we do not have the heart to eat, we will not taste the food. This proves that the heart is the controlling organ. In order to control the whole building, we must be able either to close or open the door. So, with the heart there is the power to close or open our whole being.

For this reason the preaching of the gospel must be guided by the Holy Spirit that it might hit the human heart. The most effectual way of preaching the gospel is to touch the human heart. If one can break through the heart, many persons can be gained. This is why unbelievers harden and close their heart to the gospel preaching. Regardless of how much we preach, when they close their heart, we cannot touch them. We cannot minister anything into them, because their "entrance" is closed. We must find a way, if we are going to preach effectively, to break through the entrance. The best preacher is the one who finds the key to unlock the heart.

Even the Lord Himself attracts us through our heart. He does not stir our spirit first. The seeking one in the very beginning of the Song of Solomon asks the Lord to attract her by His love so that she may love Him. The Lord comes to touch our heart with His love. This is why, after the resurrection, the Lord asked Peter, "Lovest thou me?" (John 21). The love of the Lord is the best way to unlock the door of the heart. Therefore, the most effective way to open the heart is to preach the love of God. Once the heart is open, it is easy for the Holy Spirit to touch the spirit and all the parts of man's being. This is true not only in gospel preaching, but even in the ministry of Christian teaching.

DEALING WITH THE HEART

For this reason we must deal with our heart, that we might have a proper relationship with the Lord. How can we deal with our heart? Again, it is quite simple. The Scripture says, "Blessed are the *pure* in heart" (Matt. 5:8). Some translators have changed the word "pure" to "clean"—that is, "clean in heart." But the word "clean" is not adequate. It is not just a matter of a clean heart, but of a pure heart. We may be clean, but mixed, and therefore not pure. To be mixed does not mean to be dirty, but to have more than one goal and one aim.

This is the problem with many brothers and sisters. They think that they have nothing wrong with their hearts because they are clean and without condemnation. But they are not pure, because they have more than one goal, more than one aim. Yes, they are aiming at God, but at the same time they are aiming at several other things. They may be aiming at

God *and* at a doctor's degree. When they have two things as their aims, they are mixed and complicated. For example, we cannot see two things with our eyes at the same time. If we try to look at two items at the same time, both of them will be blurred.

Why is it that some say they are not clear about the Lord's will? It is because they have two goals, two aims. Many brothers and sisters have more than two aims. They are aiming at many things. Yes, they are seeking the Lord, but at the same time they are seeking other things, such as their position and their career. How can they avoid being perplexed and confused? Their heart must be purified from so many ambitions that the Lord Himself may be their only goal.

Even many Christian workers have too many goals. One brother testified that he had a great goal: he wanted to be the biggest preacher in his denomination. His heart was clean, but he was not pure. His heart must be purified until he has only one goal—the Lord Himself. Some Christian workers have the Lord Himself *and* His work as their goal. They have two goals. They need to purify their heart until they seek nothing other than the Lord Himself as their goal. Their aim, their goal, and their interest should only be the Lord Himself. When they seek absolutely nothing but Him, their heart is pure; and if they have such a pure heart, the "sky" will not only be open but very clear to them. Sometimes the sky is open but cloudy. Why is the spiritual sky cloudy? Because the heart is mixed and not pure. When the heart is purified from many goals, the sky is clear.

Another term the Bible uses to describe the heart is "singleness"—"singleness of heart." Some versions translate singleness as simplicity—"simplicity of heart." Singleness of heart means to be simple. To be simple means, in a sense, to be foolish. Those who really love the Lord and aim at Him are a kind of fool. We must all be Christian fools! This means, "I don't know anything but Jesus. Whatever I do, I know only Jesus. Wherever I go, I know only Jesus." We should not try to be clever. We have only one way—the narrow way of Jesus. People will say, "You are foolish," but we should like to be so foolish. This is simplicity.

Three Scriptural passages referring to purity of heart are Psalms 73:1, Matthew 5:8, and 2 Timothy 2:22. The latter reference shows that while the churches are deteriorating, we must pursue the Lord with a pure heart and pray together with others who have a pure heart. There are at least three verses referring to singleness of heart: Acts 2:46, Ephesians 6:5, and Colossians 3:22. If we would seek and serve the Lord, we must deal with these two matters: to be pure and single in the heart. We must learn to have not only a clean and right heart, but a pure and single heart. If we would deal with our heart in such a way, our whole being will be opened to the Lord, because the gateway is open. This is not some doctrine, but simply instructions on how to deal with the heart so as to allow the Lord to possess our whole being.

DEALING WITH THE CONSCIENCE

Again, we repeat: the Lord must first attract us by His love. He touches our heart with His love in order to open our heart. Then, immediately following the dealings with the heart, the conscience must be dealt with. The dealings in the presence of the Lord are first with the heart and then with the conscience. If we are pure and single in our heart, the function of our conscience will immediately be very keen and alert. While we are reading this book, we may not have the sense that we are wrong and have made mistakes; but when we deal with our heart and make it pure and single, the conscience will function in a full way. Our conscience will begin to accuse us, causing us to confess and deal with it. This will make our "conscience void of offense." Paul said that he exercised himself to have a "conscience void of offense toward God and men" (Acts 24:16). A conscience void of offense means to be free from any kind of offense or accusation.

In order to know the difference between the soul and the spirit, we need a keen conscience. But this is difficult when we reason in our mentality. You say, "Well, I am wrong ten percent, but that brother wronged me one hundred percent. So he owes me a balance of ninety percent." This is nothing but mental figuration in the soul. While we are reasoning logically in our mentality, there is something deeper within us saying, "Regardless of how much he owes you, you must deal with the ten percent."

The spiritual account is not like the bank account. The account in the bank has credit, debit, and balance; but the account in the spirit has only one column, the debit. Regardless of how much credit we may have, as long as we have a debit, we must deal with it. Suppose I stole a watch from you, and you stole a car from me. We are very clear about what we stole from each other. But one day, the conscience functions: "You have to deal with that stolen article." Of course, if I were simply balancing a bank account I would reason: "This watch costs $100 and that car costs $2000, so this man owes me $1900. There is no need for me to deal with my conscience; rather, I should collect the balance." But the spiritual account does not work that way. The spiritual account demands that I forget how much the other person owes me and that I deal with the $100. I must even apologize to this man: "Sir, I am so sorry. It is sinful for me to steal. Here is the stolen watch, which I am returning to you." I must not say a word about that car! I have no right to mention it. Only the Holy Spirit has the right to say something to him. In the heavenly account there is only one column, not two.

Do you see the point? If you are arguing and reasoning, you are simply in the mind, not in the spirit.

To further illustrate, suppose the Holy Spirit is working in your spirit, demanding that you answer the call of the Lord. But a lot of reasons flood your mind: How about my wife? How about my children? What about their education? I still have a mother that is 80 years old. It is better to wait a little longer. After she dies, it will be the right time for me to answer the Lord's call. This is nothing but the arguments and rationalizations in the mentality of the soul. You are quite logical, quite reasonable, quite right, but there is still the call of the Lord deep in your spirit.

It is easy to understand the difference between the soul and the spirit, but the problem is that our whole being may still be locked, for our heart is not yet opened. We must say this again and again: we have to open our heart. When we deal with our heart so that it is pure and single, our conscience will then be very keen to make known many accusations and offenses. Our conscience, then, can only be made right by confession and by applying the sprinkling, the cleansing of the Lord's blood (Heb. 9:14).

When our conscience is cleansed, we will serve the living God. God is a living God, but He is not a living God to us when our conscience is full of offense. When this is the case, we have a God in name only; but when our conscience is cleansed by the blood, we sense that God is so living. Sometimes it seems as if God is not so real and living; He is just a title, GOD, and that's all. Then our conscience is dull and full of offenses; it needs to be dealt with by confession and cleansing.

Then we will have a pure conscience. The Apostle Paul told Timothy that he served God with a pure conscience—not only a cleansed conscience, but a conscience without any mixture and shadow (2 Tim. 1:3). An accusation in our conscience makes it impure and opaque, hindering our fellowship with the Lord.

A pure conscience is also a good conscience (1 Tim. 1:5, 19 and 1 Pet. 3:16, 21). A good conscience is a conscience that is both cleansed and purified. It is right and transparent, without any shadow. A conscience in such a good condition will bring us into the presence of the Lord. There is nothing as a barrier between us and Him, because the conscience has been cleansed and purified.

DEALING WITH THE FELLOWSHIP

Following the dealing with the conscience, the faculty of fellowship in our spirit is dealt with, as seen in 1 John 1:1-7. Fellowship between us and God is maintained by a good conscience. When the conscience is offended, it becomes a barrier and damages our fellowship with the Lord; therefore, according to 1 John 1:9, we must confess our faults, our failures, and our sins so that the blood of the Lord Jesus might cleanse our conscience. Then there will be no condemnation in our conscience to hinder our fellowship with the Lord. Strictly speaking, our fellowship is dependent upon our dealing with the conscience. It is maintained through a pure conscience.

Therefore, these two dealings are actually one, since to deal with our conscience is to deal with our fellowship. Fellowship will be maintained if there is nothing wrong in our conscience. If there is a break in our fellowship with the Lord, it means that our conscience is wrong. When our conscience is not pure and transparent, the fellowship is gone and can only be regained when our conscience is recovered.

DEALING WITH THE INTUITION

Now we come to the intuition. As the fellowship follows the conscience, so the intuition follows the fellowship. If we are wrong in the conscience, the fellowship is broken, and when the fellowship is broken, the intuition does not function. The dealing with the conscience is therefore very basic. A transparent conscience will bring us into the presence of the Lord, resulting in a living fellowship with Him. Through this living fellowship, it is easy for our spirit to sense the will of God directly—this is the function of the intuition. This function depends entirely upon a perfect fellowship. When our fellowship is perfect, the intuition functions properly. When our fellowship with the Lord is broken, automatically, the intuition does not work and can only be recovered through restored fellowship.

First John 2:27 is a very important word, which most of us neglect. It says that the anointing abideth in us. The anointing is the working of the Holy Spirit within our spirit giving us a direct sense from God. That direct sense is the intuition. First John, chapter one, indicates that the fellowship is kept or maintained by the blood. Chapter two indicates that the intuition works by the inner anointing of the Holy Spirit. When the Holy Spirit anoints us by moving in our spirit, we receive a direct sense of the intuition.

Through the intuition within our spirit we have an inner knowledge, not a mental understanding. The inner knowledge is in our spirit, while the understanding is in our mind, and the inner knowledge of our spirit always precedes the understanding of our mind. In other words, when the Holy Spirit anoints our spirit, we receive a direct sense in our intuition. Through the intuition within our spirit, we have an inner knowledge, sensing something of God. But we still need the mind to understand what we sense in the spirit. Sometimes we can only know something in the spirit, but we cannot understand it in the mind. This sounds like heavenly language, and the world does not know what we are talking about. The understanding in the mind functions only to interpret what our spirit senses as the inner knowledge. Our enlightened and renewed mind will interpret what we sense in the intuition of our spirit.

Let us put it in this way. Sometimes in the morning while reading the Word and praying, a burden is spontaneously sensed deeply within our spirit, a burden so heavy and deep that we cannot understand what it is. We have to look to the Lord for the understanding of this burden. Gradually, during the day we begin to understand with our mind what is in our spirit. In the morning we sensed the burden, or the inner knowledge, by the intuition in our spirit, but during the day we gradually receive its interpretation in our mind.

To summarize, 1 John 1 reveals that the fellowship must be maintained, and 1 John 2, especially verse 27, shows that the intuition must be stirred up or anointed by the Holy Spirit. But both the fellowship and the intuition depend entirely upon our dealing with the conscience. Through such dealing we can obtain a transparent and pure conscience, which will give us a perfect fellowship with the Lord. This will result in the function of the intuition, because the Holy Spirit will then have the ground to move and anoint our spirit. Again we say that all these things must be put into daily practice. Day by day we must deal with our heart, our conscience, our fellowship, and our intuition.

CHAPTER NINE

DEALING WITH THE SOUL

In the order of our dealings with the Lord, we must start with the heart, because it is the entrance and the exit of our whole being. Secondly, we must deal with the conscience, and, thirdly, with our fellowship with the Lord. By having a pure conscience, a conscience void of offense, we will have a transparent fellowship with the Lord. The intuition, or the anointing, is next in order and is always based upon the sprinkling of the blood. Even the Old Testament types set forth this principle. The blood always precedes the anointing: the sprinkling of the blood deals with the negative things, and the anointing of the Holy Spirit brings in the positive, applying the very element, essence, or substance of God Himself to us. The blood washes away all that is negative, and the anointing brings in all that God is. God Himself is applied to us by the anointing. By this anointing within our spirit we receive a direct sense of God through the function of the intuition. According to our Christian experience, this is the right order: the heart, the conscience, the fellowship, and the intuition. All dealings start from our heart and continue to our spirit. Now we must proceed with the dealings of the soul.

DEALING WITH THE MIND

With the intuition in our spirit, we need the mind. The intuition gives the sense of the inner knowledge. But to sense the spiritual things is one thing, and to understand them is another! The things of God are sensed in the spirit, but they are understood in the mind. Many times we know something of God within our spirit, but due to the problem of our mind we do not understand it. Sometimes it may take two or three weeks or even months before we are able to understand what we sense in our spirit. We are aware of something, but we cannot interpret it. We need the understanding in our mind to interpret what is in our spirit. The things of God are sensed by the function of the intuition in our spirit, but they are understood by the function of the understanding in our mentality.

It is for this reason we are told in Romans 12:2 that we need the renewing of the mind. But this verse first says that we are not to be conformed to this age. The "world" in the King James Version means "age" in the Greek text, and "age" here in the Greek is equivalent to the English word "modern." The age is the present, or modern, course of this world. The world's history is divided into successive ages, such as the first century, the second century, and so forth. We could say that each century is an age. Without the ages, the world could not exist. Today's age is that part of the world's system presently surrounding us; so, to be conformed to this age means that we are modern, following the present course of the world.

The verse goes on to say, "....but be ye transformed by the renewing of your mind." If we are occupied by the things of this age, our mind can never be renewed. This is why many Christians who are really saved cannot understand spiritual things. They have become too modern. We have to give up this modern age. If we are conformed to this age, we can never be transformed by the renewing of the mind.

Since the mind is a part of the soul, it is in the soul that transformation takes place. We have been regenerated in the spirit, but now the problem is the soul. There is no doubt about our regeneration, because the Lord is within us as our eternal life, and the Holy Spirit is dwelling in our spirit. Our spirit has been quickened and regenerated with Christ as life by the Holy Spirit. But what about our soul? What about our mind, our will, and our emotion? In our spirit we are entirely different from the people of the world, but I am afraid that in our mind, will, and emotion we are still exactly the same. Regeneration has been accomplished in our spirit, but after regeneration, we still need the transformation in the soul.

Let us illustrate this by a few instances. What about our clothing? Many who are saved are just like the people of the world in their thinking about fashion. They dress in conformity to this modern age. They think that as long as it is not sinful, it is quite all right, but this is merely the human thought and the natural concept. If they would be transformed by the renewing of their mind, their thoughts about their manner of dress would change.

And what about our spending? Has the way we use our money been changed? I know the story of many Christians. After they are saved, they continue to use their money in much the same way as those in the world. Not until they love the Lord more and give the Lord more ground to work within them will they be transformed in their way of spending money.

In the same way, there are many young brothers studying in the colleges who have the same thoughts about their studies and their degrees as other worldly young people. But if they would give ground to the Lord and be transformed in the soul by the renewing of their mind, their mind would be changed about these matters. This does not mean that they would give up their studies, but that their thoughts and concepts about their studies would be entirely different. They would have another point of view from which to evaluate their studies and their degrees.

There should be a change in our thoughts towards almost everything. What is this change in our thoughts? It is the transformation of our soul by the renewing of our mind. We have Christ as life within our spirit, but now we need Christ to spread into the inward parts of the soul and saturate them with Himself. This will transform our soul into His very image. The image of Christ will then be reflected in our thoughts. In whatever we think and consider, our renewed mind will express the glorious image of Christ. The understanding of our mind will then be spiritual. It will be very easy for the mind to understand the things which we sense in our spirit.

The proper translation of Romans 8:6 is, "to set the mind on the spirit is life and peace," or, "the mind set on the spirit is life and peace." In Romans 7 the mind is attempting to do things by its own independent effort; thus, it is always defeated. But in Romans 8, the mind cooperates with the spirit and is set on the spirit. The mind has found another law, which is more powerful and stronger than the law of sin mentioned in chapter 7. This new law is the law of life of the indwelling Christ in our spirit. The mind never again attempts to do things independently, but sets itself on the spirit, which is indwelt by the Holy Spirit. The mind is set on the spirit, not on the flesh. It is one thing to renew the mind, and another to set the mind upon the spirit and stand and cooperate with the spirit. The more our mind stands with our spirit, the more it will come under the control of our spirit.

Because our mind stands with the spirit, the spirit will rule over the mind, saturate the mind, and become "the spirit of our mind." Romans 8:6 says, "the mind of the spirit," but Ephesians 4:23 says, "the spirit of the mind." When the spirit controls and saturates the mind, the spirit becomes the spirit of the mind. Let us consider the context of Ephesians 4:23. Verse 22 states that we must put away the old man, and verse 24 says that we must put on the new man. This is the work of the cross and the resurrection. The putting away of the old man is the work of the cross, and the putting on of the new man is the work of resurrection. Between the work of the cross and the work of the resurrection is verse 23, "be renewed in the spirit of your mind." The renewing of the mind includes the work of the cross with the resurrection. It means that our natural mind must be crossed out and renewed in resurrection. The death of the cross is not the end, but a process leading to an end, which is resurrection. The more we die by the cross, the more we will be resurrected. The negative things will not only be put to an end, but the way will also be opened for the positive. Death to the natural mind leads to a resurrected mind. We will then have a renewed mind in resurrection. This renewed mind is in the spirit and under the control of the spirit; it is filled with the spirit and full of the spirit. Hence, the spirit becomes the spirit of the mind. Then our mind will not only be a renewed mind, but also a spiritual mind with spiritual understanding. It is easy for such a spiritual mind to interpret the spiritual things sensed by our intuition.

DEALING WITH THE WILL

Suppose our renewed mind understands what we sense by the intuition. Then the issue is our willingness to obey what we understand. We may understand, but we may also say, "No!" To obey with the will is another problem. Actually, if we do not have an obedient will, it is difficult to understand what is in the intuition. The Lord is very wise; He never does anything wastefully. If He knows that we have no willingness to obey, there is no need for us to receive the understanding. He will just leave us in darkness. Why should He allow us to understand if we will not obey? The understanding must be backed by an obedient will, ready to obey the Lord (John 7:17). When we are ready to obey, we will be able to understand.

For example, some have come to me with questions, but without a heart to listen and understand. I realized that it would just be a waste of time to talk with them. Sometimes I asked: "Do you really mean business? If I answer your question, would you obey?" Their answer would usually be, "Well, maybe, but I may not like to do it. I just want to study and find out what is what." The will must be wholly submissive, and not only submissive, but in *harmony* with the will of God (Luke 22:42, James 4:7, Phil. 2:13).

God created us with a free will. He never forces us to do anything, but always gives us the option to choose. Although He is great and wise, yet He will never force us. If He were to use force, it would mean that He is really small. Satan not only forces people, but even seduces them. But God would never do that. God says, in effect, "If you like it, do it; if you don't, don't. If you love Me, just do it. If you don't love Me, forget it. Go your own way." Thus, there is the need to exercise our will; otherwise, it is difficult for God to do anything. In order to exercise our will, we must make our will submissive and ready to obey all the time. We should not only submit ourselves to the will of God, but also bring our will into harmony with His.

When our will is dealt with to such an extent, it will be transformed. It will be saturated with Christ as our life by the spreading of the Holy Spirit. Others will sense the savor and the very image of Christ in our will. Every decision we make will be an expression of Christ. This is not a supposition, nor just a doctrine. Sometimes when we meet some dear ones in the Lord, we sense the savor of Christ in whatever they say, whatever they choose, whatever they decide. This simply proves that they have been saturated with Christ by being transformed in their will and in their mind.

DEALING WITH THE EMOTION

The last dealing of the soul is with our troublesome emotion. As we all know, nearly all our troubles are related to the emotion. It must be under the control of the Holy Spirit. This is why Matthew 10:37-39 exhorts us to love the Lord more than everything else. What the Lord does not allow, we should not love. The regulating of our love under the control of the Lord is the negative side. But we must also know the positive side, of always being ready to exercise our emotion according to the Lord's pleasure. Many, many times our emotions have the Lord's permission, but not His pleasure. He allows us to love something, but He is not pleased.

A sister once found herself in such a situation. She knew that the Lord allowed her emotion to do certain things, but she realized that the Lord was not happy. She went back to the Lord and said: "Lord, even though Thou hast permitted this, yet I will not do it. I realize that you are not happy!" This is very good. She received sweet communion and was full of peace and joy. She learned the lesson of bringing her emotion entirely under the control of the Lord and His pleasure. Sometimes we can get the Lord's permission to love something, but not His joy. The more we love it, the more we lack the joy. Finally, it becomes a suffering, not an enjoyment. This proves that we are wrong in our emotion. We all must learn to deal with our emotion according to the pleasure and joy of the Lord. If we do not sense the joy of the Lord in what we are seeking, we must not love it.

Many have heard messages from Matthew 10:37-39, exhorting them not to love their parents, their brothers and sisters, and themselves more than the Lord; but they cannot understand what this means. It simply means that they have to love everything under the control of the Lord with His pleasure. The Lord is not so small, nor is He so cruel; but we must learn that whatever we hate or love, whatever we like or dislike, must be done under the permission of the Lord with His joy. We must exercise our emotion according to the Lord's emotion. When our emotion is not under His emotion, we are wrong and can never have His joy. The more we go our own way, the more we will lose our joy. We cannot have the sweet, tender, and deep communion with the Lord. Although no one can condemn us that we are wrong, and we can even claim before others that we have received the Lord's permission, yet we realize that it is without His joy.

If our emotion is kept under the rule of the Lord with His pleasure and joy, it will be saturated with the spirit. We will then be transformed into the very image of the Lord from one stage of glory into another.

By dealing with the heart, conscience, fellowship, intuition, mind, will, and emotion, we will be mature and fully grown; we will have the stature of the Lord. All we will have to do then is to wait for His coming to transfigure our body. If our soul is transformed, spiritual strength and power will even now saturate our weak, mortal body when we need it. We will not only be regenerated in the spirit and transformed in the soul, but the divine life will also saturate our mortal body in times of physical weakness. Finally, at the coming of the Lord, the body will be transfigured and our whole being—spirit, soul, and body—will be in the glorious image of the Lord. This will be the ultimate application of the Lord's redemption, which is applied in three steps: (1) regeneration of the spirit, (2) transformation of the soul, and (3) the transfiguration of the body. At the present time we are in the process of transformation.

The soul needs all of these dealings: the dealings with the mind, with the will, and with the emotion. May the Lord help us to put these into practice. This is what the Lord's children need today. All the teachings and the gifts are given by the Lord for this purpose. It is only by this process that we can be the proper materials for the building of the Church.

Chapter Ten

THE DIGGING OF OUR INWARD
AND HIDDEN PARTS

In this chapter we will learn how to have the flow of the Spirit within our inward parts. In Numbers chapter 20, the smitten rock, which typifies Christ as smitten and riven, flowed with living water (1 Cor. 10:4). Then in chapter 21, the well dug by the people of God sprang up with water. Therefore, in these two chapters of the same book, there is first a rock which must be smitten for the living water to flow out, and then a well which must be dug for the water to spring up.

If we read the Scriptures carefully, we will realize that both the rock and the well are types of Christ, revealing Him in two different aspects. The rock typifies Christ on the cross, smitten by God so that the living water, which is the Spirit of life, may flow out into us. The well shows a different aspect. While the rock is Christ on the cross, the well is Christ within us (John 4:14). For believers, it is not a matter of the rock, but the well. Christ as the rock has already accomplished His work on the cross, which issued in the water of life flowing into us; but, today, Christ as the well of living water springing up continuously within us is something else, and has much to do with the present process of digging.

The purpose of this chapter is not to give further teaching, but to encourage us to go to the Lord to be dug. We must not talk too much about doctrines, about circumstances, about future steps, nor about guidance concerning the Lord's will. We ourselves must be dug. Why? Because I believe that even up to the present moment most of us do not have the free flow of living water. Our prayers are not so free. Our testimonies are not so strong, and in many ways we have been defeated

and are not so victorious. This is due to one thing: the flow of
the spiritual life, or the spring of the living water, is not free
within us. There is much dirt within us that must be dug out.
You may ask, "What is this dirt?" It is the dirt in our conscience, our emotion, our will, and our mind. Our hearts have
much dirt which needs to be dug out, and even in our spirit
there is some dirt which must be dealt with.

DIGGING THE CONSCIENCE

What do I mean by using the word "dirt"? It means that
our *conscience* is not so pure. Perhaps at this very moment
some accusation which we have not confessed to the Lord is
still upon our conscience. These accusations are the dirt
which needs to be dug away. The reason we do not sense
much liberty within is because of the accusations in our conscience. What are the accusations? You must ask yourself;
only you know. You know what is within you that is wrong
with others. When you are not right with others, the accusations persist. When you refuse to do what the Lord demands,
this becomes an accusation in your conscience. Then you
wonder why you are bound and without freedom. It is simply
because there is a demand of the Lord which you will not
answer, and it has become an immediate accusation in your
conscience. Your conscience is not pure from accusations and
void of offenses.

If we would experience a free, inward flow of the Spirit,
our conscience must first be dealt with and purified. The dirt
can only be dug away by going to the Lord several times each
day. I would suggest that during this week we go to the Lord
again and again, even while we are walking along the street.
We have to go to the Lord in our spirit and be dug in His
presence. By the help of the Holy Spirit we must dig away all
the dirt.

DIGGING THE HEART

After dealing with the accusations in our conscience, we
must also dig away the many things condemned by the Lord in
our *heart*. Not many brothers and sisters have a pure heart
in seeking only the Lord Himself. On one hand, many are

seeking the Lord and His way; but on the other, they are still seeking too many things other than the Lord Himself. The heart then becomes complicated and is not free and pure. We must go to the Lord once again to dig away all the things other than Christ in our heart.

You may ask, "What things need to be dug away?" Perhaps one of the first things is your concern about the future and the guidance of the Lord. You should not be bothered by this; the future is not in your hands, but in the Lord's. In fact, you should not have any future—the Lord Himself is our only future! We do not know how "sticky" our heart is. Many years ago fly paper was used to catch flies, and how sticky it was! Whatever touched it stuck to it. Our heart is just like the fly paper—so sticky. Whatever touches the heart sticks to it. These things must all be cut off. It seems that we are all seeking the Lord. Many of us are living only for the Lord and have given up our homes and our jobs. Day by day we are seeking the Lord's guidance, but we do not know how many things complicate our heart. Can we forget these things? To dig away the dirt from the conscience is easy, but to dig away the dirt from the heart is not so easy. In so many things we are kind to ourselves; we do not like to dig our heart severely. It is easy to dig away the accusations from our conscience, but it is not so easy to dig away the things that we love from our heart. We are stuck to the things we hold dearly. This is why the Scriptures tell us that we need a good conscience and a pure heart. "Blessed are the pure in heart, for they shall see God" (Matt. 5:8).

There is no doubt that we love the Lord and are seeking Him, but our loving and seeking the Lord is with a *complicated* heart. The aim and the goal of our heart are not so pure. We do not know how many goals are within our heart. What about our family? Our job? Our degree? What about this year, and next year? There are so many things still in our heart. I tell you, brothers and sisters, all this dirt is frustrating the flow of living water within us and must be dug away. Since the day we received the Lord Jesus as our Savior, He has come into us as the springing well of living water. But the problem today is that there is too much dirt in our conscience and in our heart.

DIGGING THE MIND

When someone is digging a deep well, many times he will discover that the earth is of many layers. One layer is of soft dirt, the next layer is of hard dirt, and another layer of stone. It is difficult to dig through a layer of stone. This illustrates the many layers in us through which we have to dig. We have a layer of the conscience, a layer of the heart, and now we have a layer of our *mind,* which holds much dirt. Oh, we do not know how many imaginations we have day by day! We not only dream during the night while we are asleep, but we are still dreaming during the day while we are awake. All of our imaginations are different dreams. We have already spoken about Satan blinding our minds; he does it merely by the imaginations. Sometimes while you are listening to a message, I do not know where your mind is—perhaps it has traveled to the moon! Outwardly you are nodding your head, but inwardly your mind is imagining something in space. During the message you hear the voice, but you do not receive anything. Your mind has been blinded by imaginations.

Many times people travel completely around the world in their imaginations. Within seconds, people can travel through the whole world. They can go to the Far East faster than the best jet! Oh, how many imaginations are in the mind! When there is a lot of dirt in your mind, how can the flow of living water within you be free? Since your mind has been blocked, the living water has also been blocked in your mind. The heaps of dirt are simply the many thoughts, imaginations, and dreams, which must be dug away before the living water can freely flow.

DIGGING THE WILL

The *will* also contains much dirt. There are not many who are absolutely and utterly obedient to the Lord. We need to be more submissive in our wills. Oh, how many times we do not submit ourselves to the Lord's sovereign arrangement! Sometimes we think we are quite submissive to the Lord, but when He puts us into certain circumstances, we are exposed. It is easy to submit to the invisible Lord, but it is rather difficult to submit to visible persons. You say, "Oh, I am submissive to the Lord. With the Lord I have no problem. But..." Yes, there is a big *but!* "Before the Lord I have no problem, *but with the church*...Oh, I cannot be submissive to them!" The Lord especially put you into your local church in order to break your will.

"If my husband could be such a dear brother, I would gladly be submissive to him." How many times have you sisters thought this! But the fact is that your husband cannot be that kind of person. The Lord gave you such a suitable husband; he is just the husband you need. If you could have the husband of your dreams, you would never be exposed. Many experiences and circumstances under His sovereignty simply expose us to the light, that we may know how stubborn our will is. You may point out a brother who is stubborn, but everyone of us is stubborn. We may be the *most* stubborn brothers. Everyone of us has to dig his will. How easy it is to obtain more and more spiritual knowledge, while our life, our nature, our disposition are never changed. This is utter failure! If the living water is to flow in us, we must be dug. The flowing is the Lord's business, but the digging is our business. We have to dig ourselves.

DIGGING THE EMOTION

After digging away the dirt from the will, we need to deal with our *emotion.* I do not know how to illustrate how troublesome our emotion is. The emotional problem not only exists with the sisters, but also includes the brothers. When we are emotional, we are occupied with ourselves. We are under the control and bondage of our emotions. If we would spend some time with the Lord and open ourselves, we must start by digging our conscience, then our heart, next our mind, and then our will. Finally, we will come to the point where we see how much we are still in our emotions. It is so easy for us to like one thing and dislike another. It is so easy to make friends with one brother, but the next morning to treat him as an "enemy." It is not very easy to change our will, but it is easy to have many changes in our emotions. Our emotions fluctuate even more than the weather.

This is not just a message! My deep concern is to give a little instruction so that you will go to the Lord. Forget about *your* needs, *your* jobs, *your* future, and *your* circumstances. Only seek the Lord's presence, and ask Him to bring you into His light. Then follow His light to dig away the dirt in your conscience, heart, mind, will, and emotion. The more you dig away the dirt, the more you will be alive. You will be living, you will be strengthened, and you will be victorious. This is the key to solve your many problems. You must maintain the flow of living water—that is, the fellowship of life flowing freely within you. When the living water flows freely within you, then there is victory. All the problems will be solved spontaneously and even unconsciously. Although you do not know how to solve them, yet they will be solved by the flowing of the living water, the fellowship of life. This flowing of the living water is entirely dependent upon your digging.

This digging is only accomplished by prayer. We have to spend more and more time with the Lord and pray according to His inner leading. According to that leading, we must confess and dig away all the dirt within us. I believe these instructions are clear; now we need to practice them. Sometimes we need to pray with others, but the digging prayer is more prevailing in privacy. It is extremely necessary to spend more private time with the Lord. All the dirt within the conscience, heart, mind, will, and emotion must be dug away by our prayers. You may say, "I am so busy." But, although we are busy with the duties of the day, we can still touch the Lord and dig away the dirt. Many times while I am working, I apply myself to the digging exercise. We should learn to pray, to contact the Lord, and to dig away all the inward dirt.

> Spring up, well, with water.
> Dig Thou, Lord, completely;
> Dig away all barriers
> That Thy stream flow through me.

Christ, the Rock, is riven;
Living water's flowing;
But within my heart now
It is blocked from going.

I will dig by praying,
Dig the dirt entirely,
Thus release the Spirit,
Let the stream flow freely.

There's no need again that
Christ, the Rock, be riven,
But unto the digging
That I should be given.

What I need most deeply
Is the Spirit's filling,
That the living water
From my heart be welling.

Dig till there is nothing
Left to block the passage;
Dig until the stream flows
With the living message.

Spring up, well, with water.
Dig Thou, Lord, completely;
Dig away all barriers
That Thy stream flow through me.

Hymn #250 in *Hymns*.

CHAPTER ELEVEN

DISCERNING THE SPIRIT FROM THE SOUL

"Now the natural man receiveth not the things of the Spirit of God: for they are foolishness unto him; and he cannot know them, because they are spiritually judged" (1 Cor. 2:14).

"Natural" here is an important word in the Greek text, meaning "soulish"; therefore, the "natural man" really means the "soulish man." The following verse in this passage of Scripture discloses another kind of man: "But he that is spiritual judgeth all things" (1 Cor. 2:15). The soulish man is seen in verse 14 and the spiritual man in verse 15. These verses tell us very clearly that the soulish man cannot receive the spiritual things of God. Only the spiritual man can discern them.

"Then said Jesus unto his disciples, If any man would come after me, let him deny himself, and take up his cross, and follow me. For whosoever would save his life shall lose it: and whosoever shall lose his life for my sake shall find it. For what shall a man be profited, if he shall gain the whole world, and forfeit his life? or what shall a man give in exchange for his life?" (Matt. 16:24-26).

Three things are emphasized in verse 24: first, "deny himself"; next, "take up the cross"; and finally, "follow me." The "me" is Christ in the Holy Spirit, who now indwells us. In verses 25 and 26, the Greek word for "life" is the same one for "soul." Hence, they may be rendered: "whosoever will save his *soul* shall lose it, and whosoever shall lose his *soul* for my sake shall find it. For what shall a man be profited, if he shall gain the whole world, and forfeit his *soul?* or what shall a man give in exchange for his *soul?*" We have to lose our soul. In other words, we must deny the self.

"And he said unto all, If any man would come after me,
let him deny himself, and take up his cross daily, and follow
me. For whosoever would save his life shall lose it; but whosoever shall lose his life for my sake, the same shall save it.
For what is a man benefited, if he gain the whole world, and
lose or forfeit his own self?" (Luke 9:23-25).

Here Luke adds a word which Matthew 16:24-26 does not
give, the word "daily"—i.e., one must "take up his cross *daily.*"
These verses also say "lose his own self" instead of "lose his
soul." This proves, therefore, that "soul" in Matthew is the
same as "self" in Luke.

"Brethren, even if a man be overtaken in any trespass,
ye who are spiritual, restore such a one in a spirit of gentle-
ness" (Gal. 6:1).
"The grace of our Lord Jesus Christ be with your spirit"
(Gal. 6:18).
"The grace of our Lord Jesus Christ be with your spirit"
(Philemon 25).

In these verses, it says "your spirit"; hence, this is the
human spirit.

"And if Christ is in you, the body is dead because of sin;
but the spirit is life because of righteousness" (Rom. 8:10).
"That the ordinance of the law might be fulfilled in us,
who walk not after the flesh, but after the Spirit" (Rom. 8:4).
"But I say, Walk by the Spirit, and ye shall not fulfill the
lust of the flesh. For the flesh lusteth against the Spirit, and
the Spirit against the flesh; for these are contrary the one to
the other; that ye may not do the things that ye would" (Gal.
5:16,17).

The King James Version capitalizes "Spirit" in these
verses, but in the Greek interlinear text it is not capitalized.
The reference is to the human spirit.

REVIEWING GOD'S ECONOMY

I wish to point out God's economy and its mark again. We
have seen clearly in the last few chapters that God's economy
is to dispense Himself into us. The way God dispenses Himself into us is by the Father being embodied in the Son, and
the Son being realized in the Spirit. In other words, the
Father is in the Son, and the Son is in the Spirit. Not only is

the Person of the Son in the Holy Spirit, but also the accomplished work of the Son. Therefore, the Holy Spirit includes God the Father, God the Son, the divine and human natures, the human life of Christ with the enduring power of earthly sufferings, the effectiveness of Christ's death, the resurrection power, the ascension, and the enthronement. All these elements are combined together as an "all-inclusive dose" in the Holy Spirit. It is through this all-sufficient Holy Spirit that the fullness of the Triune God has been dispensed to us.

This all-inclusive Spirit is now in our human spirit. In the type of the tabernacle or temple, there are three parts: the outer court, the holy place, and the Holiest of all. In this Old Testament figure, the Shekinah glory of God and the ark are clearly shown to be in the Holiest of all. Therefore, God's presence and Christ are neither in the outer court nor in the holy place, but in the Holiest of all. The three parts of the temple correspond to the three parts of man—the body, the soul, and the spirit. The New Testament declares that we are the temple of God and that Christ is with our spirit. "The Lord be with thy spirit" (2 Tim. 4:22). There are two verses proving that the Holy Spirit today is working with our spirit: "The Spirit himself beareth witness with our spirit, that we are the children of God" (Rom. 8:16); "But he that is joined unto the Lord is one spirit" (1 Cor. 6:17). The Lord Himself is the Spirit, each one of us has a spirit, and these two are mingled as one spirit. This proves that the Lord today dwells in our spirit. If we desire to enjoy Christ fully, we must know how to discern our spirit. For this very reason Hebrews 4:12 tells us that our spirit must be divided from our soul. Hebrews also tells us to enter the Holiest of all, which is our human spirit. If Christ is to be enjoyed as our divine portion, we must know how to enter into this Holiest place, our human spirit.

In the past centuries a number of books have been written about the book of Hebrews. We believe that the best was written by Andrew Murray, who entitled his book, *The Holiest of All.* The title is correct, for Hebrews reveals how we may enter the Holiest of all, the human spirit, where Christ dwells. It is in the spirit that Christ is everything.

If we desire to partake of Christ, we need to locate Him. You may say that He is in heaven. Without a doubt, that is right, but if He is only in heaven, how could He be enjoyed here on earth? Praise the Lord, He is not only in heaven, but at the same time He is also within us. For example, the electricity in our home is the *same* electricity in the generator far away from our home. Romans 8:34 says that Christ is in heaven at the right hand of God, but the same chapter says that Christ is in us (verse 10). In just one chapter the same Christ in heaven is also in us. If He is only in heaven and not in us, how could we experience and enjoy Him? Praise the Lord, today Christ is not only in the heavens, but also in our spirit!

Christ in our spirit is the *mark* of God's economy. God's economy is to dispense Himself into man as the all-inclusive Triune God, and the *mark* of His economy is the indwelling Christ within our spirit. Whenever we turn into our spirit, there we will meet Christ. For example, if electricity has been installed in my house and I wish to use it, what shall I do? The answer, of course, is simply to turn on the switch. Our switch is the human spirit. Many Christians can recite John 3:16, but they are ignorant of 2 Timothy 4:22, which is just as important as John 3:16—"The Lord be with thy spirit." God so loved us that He gave His only begotten Son, and we have received Him (John 1:12). We have believed in Him and received Him—but where is He? Into what part of us has He come? For so many years we have had this Treasure, but were ignorant of the fact that He was within our spirit. But now, praise Him, we know. Christ, the only begotten Son of God, is within our spirit.

DENYING THE SOUL

Although the Lord is in our spirit, our spirit is very much stuck to our soul. This is why the writer of Hebrews tells us that our spirit must be divided from our soul by the Word of God. Just as the marrow is encased within the bone and the bone must be broken before it can be seen, so our spirit, where Christ dwells, is so much sealed within the soul that our soul must be broken before it can be revealed. For this reason the Lord told us many times that we need to lose our soul and deny our self. In all four Gospels the Lord Jesus exhorts us to lose the soul, forfeit the soul, and deny the self. The soul must be denied because it has covered up the spirit. There is only one way to get to the marrow—by breaking and crushing the bones and the joints. The Lord is in our spirit, and His grace is in our spirit, but the way to Him is by crushing the soul day by day.

What is the soul? As we have already pointed out, the soul is simply the self. The self is the very center of the human being and is the human being, and it is the self which must be crossed out. We should not cross out others and put others on the cross, but put our own soul on the cross. If any man will follow Christ, he must deny his soulish life and take up his cross daily. Not just yesterday, or just today, but day by day we have to apply the cross to the soul. With so many Christians there is nothing but their ego. From the first word to the last, it is always I...I...I. But the Christian life is "no longer I, but Christ that lives in me." How could it be "no longer I, but Christ"? By having the "I" crucified. I have been put on the cross, and the cross is now on me. I have been crossed out, so there is no more I. Whenever I conversed as a young Christian, I was in the habit of using the word "I." But, praise the Lord, in these days I dare not use the word "I," but always "we." Not only "I," but also many others—including Christ!

If any man would follow Christ, he has to do three things: deny the "I," take up the cross daily, and follow Christ, who now is not only in heaven but in us. It is easy to follow Him when we first deny the self and apply the cross. *To deny the soul means that we turn from ourselves to the spirit.* Then in the spirit we will meet Christ. Why do the four Gospels tell us negatively to deny the soul, while later all the Epistles tell us positively to live and do things in me spirit? Because today the Lord Jesus is in the spirit, and His grace is in the spirit. To follow Christ is a matter of dealing with the spirit, and this is the mark of God's economy! Oh, we need to stress again this mark of God's economy! We all must be clear that God's eternal plan is to dispense Himself into our spirit. He has done this already, for He is now in our spirit to be our life and everything. All our needs are met in this wonderful Spirit who is in our spirit.

ABIDING IN THE SPIRIT

After we were saved, we were given too much religious teaching. We were taught many things: that God is the Creator and we are the creatures; that we have to fear God, serve Him, and please Him; that we must try our best to do good; and that we have to do something to glorify His name. These were the kind of teachings we received. There is nothing wrong with these religious teachings; in a sense they are good. But they are not related to the mark of God's economy.

Many of us have also received ethical teachings, such as: we have to be good, humble, patient, nice, and loving; we must not lose our temper, and we have to honor our parents; husbands must love their wives, and wives must submit to their husbands. These are the good, ethical teachings.

But, listen. This is what the Lord told us to do: "Abide in Me and I in you. I am the vine, ye are the branches. As the branches, you have to abide in Me." Forget about the religious and ethical teachings. Just remember one thing: you are a branch of Christ. Abide in Him and let Him abide in you. But if we are going to abide in Christ, we must know where Christ is. If we are going to abide in a house, we must first know where the house is located. Can we abide in Christ by abiding in the mind or in the emotion? No, we can abide in Christ only by abiding in the spirit. The Lord Himself and His grace are in our spirit. Thus, in order to abide in Christ we must discern our spirit. When we abide in Him in the spirit, He will have the opportunity to take possession of us. He will then have the ground to fill and occupy us. All of His riches will be wrought out through our spirit, and we will bear fruit to glorify Him. This is not a religious or ethical teaching; this is life in Christ.

The purpose of this book is not to give teachings, nor cause us to be more religious and ethical. No! It is to help us realize God's eternal purpose of dispensing Himself into us as our only portion, as our life and as our everything. Let us henceforth live by Him and enjoy Him as our all. Where is the key, i.e., the mark? It is in our spirit. Such a wonderful all-inclusive, unlimited God has limited Himself to dwell in our spirit. How small and how limited we are, yet God is within us, dwelling in our spirit. This is not a matter of teaching someone to be religious or ethical; it is the Triune God becoming everything to us in our spirit. Therefore, we must learn to discern our spirit, deny our soul all the time and turn continually into our spirit. We must forget our surroundings and abide in Him, and let Him abide in us. Then fruit will become the outworking of the inner life, which is Christ Himself in our spirit.

The religious way for us to be a Christian is to rise up early in the morning and pray: "Lord, I thank you for this new day. Help me today to do what is right and not to do anything wrong. Help me today to glorify Thy name and do Thy will. Lord, Thou knowest my temper is not good. Help me not to lose my temper. Lord, how nice it is to be so patient and humble. Oh, Lord, help me to be patient and humble." Perhaps we did not pray exactly in this way, but in principle this is just the way we have prayed. This is not a spiritual prayer, but a religious, ethical prayer. You may ask me, "How, then, shall I pray in the morning?" Well, I would suggest that you say: "Lord, I praise Thee. Thou art the wonderful One with the Father in the Spirit, and, oh, how glorious it is that Thy Spirit is in my spirit! Lord, I look to Thee, I behold Thee, I worship Thee! I thank Thee and praise Thee! I fellowship with Thee!" Forget about being religious and doing good. For the whole day, you will be in the heavenlies! There is no need for you to think, "Be careful, don't rush, don't lose your temper." But just pray, "Lord, I do not know any temper, any humility, any patience, any this or that; I only know Thee, the glorious Christ, the all-inclusive Christ!" Fellowship with Him, praise Him, and sing Hallelujahs! Then you will see the victory. When you come to the church meeting in the evening, you will be in the heavenlies. It will be so easy for you to release your spirit and release the spirit of others. This is the *mark* of God's economy!

Make it your responsibility not to miss the mark. Here is a map with clear instructions. There is no need for you to miss the way. Why stick to a mule wagon when today you have a jet, and not only a jet, but a rocket! Oh, I wish to tell you where the rocket is—it is in your spirit. When you turn to the spirit, it is much more than being in a new Ford! It is like being in a jet! And sometimes, in the morning, it is just like a rocket! You feel as if you are in the third heaven, so transcendent! This is not a joke! A real Christian should have such wonderful experiences of Christ as these. When you cannot endure a difficult situation and the suppression is beyond your strength, turn to your spirit and look unto Jesus. You will rise far above it, transcendent and victorious. Everything will be under your feet.

Many times I have been in trouble, not knowing what to do or what decision to make. The more I analyzed the situation, the more confused and complicated I became. Then I said: "Lord, let me forget all this. Let me come back to the spirit and look to Thee." Oh, the enlightening when we do this is so glorious! The all-inclusive One is right here in our spirit. *Abide in Me and I in you*—this is the secret. When we discern the spirit, then we can abide in Him and find that He is the all-inclusive Triune God. He is the wonderful, all-inclusive, all-sufficient Spirit indwelling our spirit. Whenever we return to our spirit to contact Him, we are in the light, we are in the life, we are in the power, we are in the heavenlies, we are with the Triune God and the Triune God is with us. How glorious! This is not just a teaching, but a real testimony of what I enjoy and experience all the time. Learn to aim at the goal of God's economy and never swerve away. Always keep to this mark to fellowship with Him, look to Him, and behold and reflect Him day by day by denying the soul and exercising the spirit.

CHAPTER TWELVE

MAN AND THE TWO TREES

God's eternal plan. His economy, is revealed to us throughout the sixty-six books of the Scriptures. At the very beginning of the Scriptures, God is seen creating man as the center of the whole creation for the purpose of expressing Himself. In His economy God intended that man should express Himself as the center of His whole universe.

MAN NEUTRAL BETWEEN THE TWO TREES

At the beginning of the Word of God, we are shown two trees, the tree of life and the tree of the knowledge of good and evil (Gen. 2). In order to understand God's plan in Scripture, we must be thoroughly clear about these two trees and what they represent. After God created man, He placed him before these two trees, and man's whole life and walk was pictured as a matter of feasting upon one tree or the other. God instructed man to be very careful about partaking of these two trees. If man dealt with them in a proper way, he would have life; otherwise, he would have death. It was a matter of life or death. How man would live and walk after his creation depended entirely upon how he dealt with these two trees. God instructed man clearly: if he partook of the second tree, the tree of the knowledge of good and evil, he would have death; but if he partook of the first tree, the tree of life, he would have life.

What do these two trees signify? According to the revelation of the whole Scripture, the tree of life signifies God Himself in Christ as our life. The tree of life stands as a symbol of the life of God in Christ. The Old and New Testaments present the Lord Jesus many times as either a "tree" or a "branch" of a tree. The Lord has the special title of "Branch" in Isaiah, Jeremiah, and Zechariah. Many trees are also used in Scripture to signify that Christ is our portion and our enjoyment. For instance, the Lord Jesus, in the second chapter of the Song of Solomon, is likened to an apple tree: "As the apple-tree among the trees of the wood, so is my beloved among the sons. I sat down under His shadow (the apple tree) with great delight." We can sit under Him as the shade—under His covering and shadow—and enjoy all His riches, the fruit of the tree. Another example of Christ as a tree is the vine-tree in John 15: "I am the vine, ye are the branches..."

What is the significance of the second tree, the tree of the knowledge of good and evil? This tree represents nothing else than Satan, the source of death. The second tree brings death, because it is the very source of death. The first tree is the source of life, and the second tree is the source of death. In the whole universe only God Himself is the source of life, and only Satan is the source of death. A verse showing that God Himself is the very source of life is Psalm 36:9: "For with thee is the fountain of life"; and a verse showing that Satan is the source of death is Hebrews 2:14: "him that had the power of death." The power of death is in the hand of Satan. Thus, from the very beginning of time, these two trees represent two sources—one, the source of life, and the other, the source of death.

In the beginning, there were three parties—God, man, and Satan. Man in innocence, created by God, was neutral to life and death. Since it was possible for man to have either life or death, he was standing on neutral ground. But God was standing on the ground of life, and Satan on the ground of death. Man was created neutral to God and Satan. It was God's intention for this neutral, innocent man to take God into himself, that God and man, man and God, would be mingled together as one. Man would then contain God as his life and express God as everything. Created man, as the center of the universe, would then fulfill the purpose of fully expressing God. Another possibility, however, was that man would be induced to take the second tree, the source of death. As a consequence, man would then be mingled with the second tree. Oh, that our eyes might be opened to see that in the whole universe it is not a matter of ethics and of doing good, but a matter of either receiving God as life or Satan as death. We must be delivered from the ethical and moral understanding. It is not a matter of doing good or evil, but of receiving God as life or Satan as death. It is important that we clearly see these three parties! God, standing on one side, is the source of life, as represented by the tree of life; Satan, standing on the side, is the source of death, as represented by the tree knowledge; and Adam, standing in the middle, is neutral with two receiving hands. He can either take God at his right hand or Satan at his left.

MAN CORRUPTED BY THE TREE OF DEATH

But, as we know, Adam was induced to take the second source, the tree of knowledge, into himself. This was not a matter of merely doing something wrong. No! It was much more serious than transgressing God's law and regulation. The significance of Adam taking the fruit of the tree of knowledge was that he received Satan into himself. Adam did not take a branch of that tree, he took the *fruit* of the tree. The fruit contains the reproducing power of life. For example, when the fruit of a peach tree is planted in the earth, soon another little peach tree will sprout up. Adam was the "earth." When he took the fruit of the tree of knowledge into himself as the earth, he received Satan, who then grew in him. Oh, this is not a small matter! Not many Christians have realized the fall of Adam in such a way. The fruit of Satan was sown in Adam as a seed in the soil; thus, Satan grew in Adam and became a part of him.

Now we need to discover into what part of Adam Satan was taken. Satan not only came into Adam when he fell in the garden, but he still remains in the human race. Where is he located in the human race? As we have seen in these chapters, we are a tripartite being: spirit, soul, and body. Look at the picture. When Adam took the fruit of the tree, into what part of his being did it come? Of course, it came into his body, because he ate it. Although this is logical and reasonable, we

need Scriptural ground to confirm that something of Satan is
in our body. Read Romans 7:23: "But I see a different law in
my members, warring against the law of my mind." The word
"another," in the King James Version, is not a good translation. It should be a "different law" —i.e., a law of a *different*
category. You may have three laws of the *same* category,
e.g. the first, and "another" two. But the Greek here means a
law of a contrasting category. "But I see a different law in my
members (the members are the parts of the body), warring
against the law of my mind, and bringing me into captivity
under the law of sin which is in my members," that is, the
parts of the body.

What is the law of sin? Paul said, "...no more I, but sin
that dwelleth in me" (Rom. 7:20), and, "...no longer I, but
Christ liveth in me" (Gal. 2:20). Here we have the contrast
between "no more I, but sin," and "no longer I, but Christ."
Christ is the embodiment of God, but sin is the embodiment
of Satan. The word "sin" in Romans 7 should be capitalized,
for it is personified. It is like a person, for Sin can dwell in us
and force us to do things against our will (Rom. 7:17, 20). It is
even stronger than us. Romans 6:14 says: "For sin shall not
have dominion over you." It is better to translate it: "For
Sin shall not have the lordship over you," or, "For Sin shall
not be lord over you." Sin can be lord over us; hence, Sin must
be the evil one, Satan. Through the fall, Satan came into man
as Sin, and is ruling, damaging, corrupting, and mastering
him. In what part? Satan is in the members of man's body.

Man's body as originally created by God was something
very good, but it has now become the flesh. The body was
pure, since it was created good, but when the body was corrupted by Satan, it became flesh. Paul said, "...in me, that is,
in my flesh, dwelleth no good thing" (Rom. 7:18). By the fall,
Satan came to dwell in our body, causing our body to become
flesh—i.e., a damaged, ruined body.

The book of Romans uses two terms, "the body of sin" (6:6)
and "the body of death" (7:24). The body is called "the body of
sin" because Sin is in the body. The body simply became the
residence of Sin, which is the embodiment of Satan. What,
then, is "the body of death"? The source and power of death is

Satan. Sin is the embodiment of Satan and death is the issue or effect of Satan. This corrupted, transmuted body is called the "body of sin," and the "body of death," because this body became the very residence of Satan. Both sin and death are related to Satan. "The body of sin" means that the body is sinful, corrupted, and enslaved by Sin; "the body of death" means that the body is weakened and full of death. The body is something satanic and devilish, because Satan dwells in this body. All the lusts are in this corrupted body which is called the flesh. The Word reveals that the lust is "the lust of the flesh" (Gal. 5:16). The flesh is the corrupted body full of lusts, indwelt by Satan. Now you see that the fall of man was not just a matter of man committing something against God, but of man *receiving Satan into his body*. Satan, from the time of the fall, dwells in man. This is what happened when man partook of the second tree.

Since Satan and man became one through the second tree, Satan is no longer outside of man, but *in* man. The prince of the air, Satan himself, is working in the disobedient people (Eph. 2:2). Satan was joyful, boasting that he had succeeded in taking over man. But God, who was still outside of man, seemed to say: "I will also become incarnated. If Satan wrought himself into man, then let Me enter man and put man upon Myself." Do you see the complicated situation? God put on this man—Satan being in him—through incarnation. When God became incarnated as a man, the kind of man He put on was a man corrupted by Satan. Man, at the time of His incarnation, was no longer a pure man, but a man ruined, corrupted by Satan. Let us read Romans 8:3: "God, sending his own Son in the likeness of the flesh of sin"—not "the sinful flesh," as in the King James Version, but "the flesh of sin." When the Lord Jesus incarnated Himself in flesh, He was "in the likeness of the flesh of sin." There was no sin within Him, but there was "the *likeness* of the flesh of sin." Sin was within the corrupted man, but there was no sin within the Lord Jesus; there was only the *likeness* of the flesh of sin. The Old Testament illustrates this in the type of the brass serpent on the pole. That serpent, made of brass, was a type of Christ (John 3:14). When Christ was on the cross, He was a man in the "the *likeness*" of the serpent. The serpent is Satan, the devil, the enemy of God, but when Christ was incarnated as a man, He had even the *likeness* of the sinful flesh, which is the likeness of Satan. It is rather difficult for anyone to understand this easily. It is really quite complicated. Let me repeat. Man was made pure, but one day Satan came into man to possess him. Satan was joyful, thinking he had succeeded in taking over man. Then God put upon Himself the man with Satan within him.

MAN RELEASED FROM THE TREE OF DEATH

After God became a man and put that man with Satan within him upon Himself, He brought that man to the cross. Satan thought he had succeeded, but he only gave the Lord an easy way to put him to death. For example, if a mouse is loose in a house, it is rather difficult for the owner to catch it. But if he sets a trap with a little bait, the mouse will then be tempted to catch the bait. The mouse at first will think he has succeeded in getting the bait, but will not realize that he has been trapped until it is too late. Then, since he is trapped, it is so easy for the owner of the house to come and put him to death. Similarly, Adam became a trap to catch Satan. Satan was the "naughty" mouse running loose in the universe. When Satan came to possess man, he thought he was so successful, but did not realize that he fell into a trap. Satan thought man was his home, but did not know that man was a trap. He thought man was his food, but man was only the bait. By taking man, he was caught and imprisoned in man. Subsequently, the Lord came and put man upon Himself to bring him to the cross, that "through death he might bring to nought him that had the power of death" (Heb. 2:14). Man was the trap, and the devil was trapped within him. Through incarnation God put the corrupted man upon Himself and brought this man to death on the cross. At the same time, Satan within this fallen man was put to death also. Thus, it is by this death on the cross that Christ destroyed the devil. This is why Satan is afraid of the cross, and this is why the Lord told us to take up the cross. The cross is the only weapon for us to overcome Satan.

Where is Satan? Satan is in me—in my flesh. But where is my flesh now? Look at Galatians 5:24: "...crucified the flesh with the passions and lusts." My flesh, with Satan in it, is on the cross; thus, Satan is put to death on the cross. Praise the Lord! But is this the end? No, burial follows death. But even the grave is not the end! After the burial, there was the resurrection. Israel went into the Red Sea *with* Pharaoh and his army, but they were resurrected from the death-water *without* Pharaoh and his army. Pharaoh and his army were buried in the death-water. Christ brought man *with* Satan into death and the grave and brought man *without* Satan out of death and the grave. He left Satan buried in the grave. Now this resurrected man is one with Christ.

MAN RESURRECTED BY THE TREE OF LIFE

Let me ask you, When was it that you were regenerated? In 1958? That's too late! You were regenerated by the resurrection of Christ (1 Pet. 1:3). When Christ was resurrected, we too, those who believe in Him, were also resurrected. This can be proven by Ephesians 2:5, 6: God has "...made us alive together with Christ, and raised us up with him." At the time of Christ's resurrection, we also were resurrected with Him. Oh, we must be impressed! Man was ruined by Satan when Satan came into him. But God, by incarnation, put this man with Satan within him *upon* Himself, brought this man to the cross, put this man including Satan to death, and buried this man in the grave. He then brought man into resurrection, and through this resurrection man with God became one. By incarnation God came into man, and by resurrection man with God became one. Now God is in man's spirit.

We have to be joyful—but not overly joyful. Why? Because we must always bear the cross daily. Whenever our flesh is away from the cross, we will find that Satan is alive again. We have to say "Hallelujah," because the Lord Jesus is in our spirit; but we must also be on the alert, for we are still in this flesh. When the flesh gets off the cross, the devil will be alive again. This is why we must live in the spirit all the time and apply the cross to the flesh. Though Satan by the fall got into man, he was dealt with by the Lord, and now by the resurrection the Lord is within us. From now on our responsibility and business is not to try to do anything good. Good will only deceive and blind us. We must simply follow the Lord in the spirit and apply the cross to the flesh. This will spontaneously put Satan to death. Learn to practice this one thing with these two aspects. Follow the Lord in the spirit, and put the flesh, including Satan, to death on the cross.

Then what will be the ultimate issue? Simply this—on the one hand, there will be the New Jerusalem, and on the other, the Lake of Fire. The New Jerusalem is the Triune God mingled together with the resurrected man, and the Lake of Fire is Satan's ultimate destruction. The Lake of Fire is the place for Satan. All which is not related to the Triune God and the resurrected man will be put into the Lake of Fire with Satan. There will be only one tree in the New Jerusalem—the tree of life. The other tree will be in the Lake of Fire. This is the ultimate conclusion of the whole Scripture. The Scripture began with three parties, but the ultimate consummation will be the New Jerusalem with only the first tree at the center of the city and the resurrected man as the expression of the Triune God. The second tree will be cast into the Lake of Fire. All things and all people related to the second tree will have the same destiny as Satan—in that Lake of Fire.

In conclusion, the meaning of this picture to us today is that the normal Christian life does not consist in doing good. The normal Christian life is simply taking Christ and living by Christ and putting the flesh with Satan to death all the time. It is to follow Christ in our spirit and to put our flesh to death. Then the day will come when the Triune God and the resurrected man will be one expression—the New Jerusalem with the tree of life as its center.

CHAPTER THIRTEEN

THE CROSS AND THE SOUL LIFE

These chapters deal with the basics of God's economy and its mark. We are not touching here upon some unimportant teachings, but upon the basic things of God's economy—not merely in the way of doctrine, but in the way of *experience.* God in His economy intends to dispense Himself into us, which He has already accomplished in the human spirit. The Triune God has been dispensed into us. It is for this purpose that God created us in three parts: body, soul, and spirit. This tripartite being is God's temple. God's temple consists of three parts: the outer court, the holy place, and the Holiest of all, the very place where God's Shekinah glory and God's Christ dwelt. The three parts of our being correspond exactly with the three parts of the temple—the body with the outer court, the soul with the holy place, and the spirit with the Holiest of all. Today, God in Christ is dwelling in our spirit, the Holiest of all.

THE TRIUNE GOD SPREADING WITHIN MAN

God's economy is to dispense Himself into our spirit as His abode and to take His residence in our spirit as a base to spread Himself through our whole being. Our spirit is His home, His dwelling place, His habitation, the very place from which He spreads Himself through our whole being. By spreading Himself through us, He saturates every part of our being with Himself. First, He thoroughly mingles Himself with our spirit, then, with the soul, and lastly, with the body. He comes into our spirit to start the mingling by regenerating our spirit. Regeneration is the mingling of God Himself with our spirit. After regeneration, if we cooperate with Him, offering ourselves to Him and giving Him the opportunity, He will spread Himself from our spirit into our soul to renew all the parts of our soul. This is His transforming work. Through transformation the very essence of the Triune God is mingled with our soul, our very self. When our soul is transformed into the image of the Lord, our thoughts, our desires, and our decisions will always express the Lord.

God's first step, therefore, is to regenerate our spirit; His second step is to transform our soul; and finally, the last step is to transfigure, or change, our body at the second coming of the Lord. The Lord will then permeate our body and His glory will saturate our whole being. This transfiguration is the ultimate consummation of His mingling with our being to the uttermost. At that time God's economy of dispensing Himself into us will be fully accomplished. Remember these three steps by which God mingles Himself with us in every way. This hymn expresses the final consummation.

> Christ is the hope of glory, my very life is He,
> He has regenerated and saturated me;
> He comes to change my body by His subduing might
> Like to His glorious body in glory bright!
>
> *Chorus*
>
> He comes, He comes, Christ comes to glorify me!
> My body He'll transfigure, like His own it then will be.
> He comes, He comes, redemption to apply!
> As Hope of glory He will come, His saints to glorify.
>
> Christ is the hope of glory, He is God's mystery;
> He shares with me God's fulness and brings God into me.
> He comes to make me blended with God in every way,
> That I may share His glory with Him for aye.
>
> Christ is the hope of glory, redemption full is He;
> Redemption to my body, from death to set it free.
> He comes to make my body a glorious one to be
> And swallow death forever in victory.
>
> Christ is the hope of glory, He is my history:
> His life is my experience, for He is one with me.
> He comes to bring me into His glorious liberty,
> That one with Him completely I'll ever be.
>
> Hymn #949 in *Hymns.*

THE TWO PARTIES FIGHTING
FOR THE SOUL

We all know the sad story. Before the glorious God came into the spirit, Satan, the enemy of God, came into us first. The devil came into the human body through Adam when he ate the fruit of the tree of knowledge. Consequently, Sin, personified as a person, is dwelling in the members of our body and rules as an illegal master, forcing us to do things we dislike. This is the sin mentioned in Romans, chapters 6, 7, and 8. It is none other than the evil, sinful one of the whole universe. He is the enemy of God. When he came into our body, our body was transmuted, or changed in nature, and thus became the *flesh*. The flesh is the corrupted, ruined, and damaged body, with the evil one dwelling in it. This flesh, therefore, threatens to dominate the soul.

As the human spirit becomes a base from which God can spread Himself, so the same principle is true with this corrupted body. The flesh, possessed by Satan, becomes the base from which he can do his devilish work. Satan takes his place in the flesh to influence the soul, and then through the soul to deaden the spirit. The direction of all satanic work always begins from the outside and works toward the inside. But the divine work always starts from the center and spreads toward the circumference. We may illustrate it in this way:

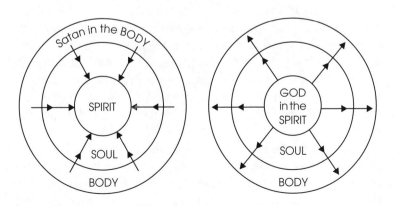

The soul cannot stand against Satan, who is much stronger than the human soul. Our condition before we were saved is that the soul was poisoned by Satan through the flesh. When we heard the gospel and were enlightened in the mind and in the conscience, we became contrite and broken in spirit, repented, and opened ourselves to the Lord; whereupon He gloriously came into our spirit to be our life in the Holy Spirit. Although Satan, the enemy, has taken the flesh as a base from which to fight inwardly toward the spirit, the glorious Lord uses the spirit as a base from which to fight outwardly toward the flesh.

We are so complicated, because we have become a battlefield! We are the universal battlefield for the universal battle. Satan and God, God and Satan, are fighting one another within us day by day. Satan is fighting toward the center, while God is fighting toward the circumference. What is our attitude? We cannot be neutral; we have to take sides. In the outward part of man is the enemy of God, and in the inward part is God Himself. Between the two, in the middle, is the soul. Satan is in the corrupted body, God is in the regenerated spirit, and we are between in the human soul. We are a very important person. We can change the whole situation. If we take sides with Satan, God, in a sense, will be defeated. Of course, God can never be defeated, but by our taking sides with Satan, it seems that God is temporarily defeated. But if we take sides with God, it will be glorious, and Satan will be utterly defeated.

With whom will you take sides? This is the problem. Listen to the Lord: "If any man would come after me, let him deny himself." Deny the self! In other words, put the soul to death on the cross, for the soul is the self. We must always deny the self, always put the self to death, always cross out the self. What will happen when the soul has been crossed out? When the soul has been put to death, only God and Satan are left. By crossing out the soul, we have burned the bridge for the enemy.

Satan is in the flesh, because he is Sin incarnated in the flesh, and self is in the soul. Both Sin and self are illegally married to each other; in fact, they had their wedding day long ago. All the trouble within us is due to the fact that self is married to Sin and they have become one. But when we were saved, God, Christ and the Holy Spirit came into our spirit as the divine life. In the flesh, the corrupted body, there is Sin; in the soul, the threatened soul, there is the self; while in the regenerated human spirit is the divine life, the eternal life, which is the regulating life and power. To live and walk by the soulish life means to live and walk by ourselves, which involves us in marriage with Satan. This marriage means that we are not a free person, but under the bondage of the evil one, Sin. The evil one in the flesh will rise up to snatch and defeat us and bring us under his captivity, making us a most wretched person. If, however, we deny the soul, the self, and live and walk by the spirit, Christ as life will regulate and saturate our whole being.

THE CROSS DEALING WITH THE SOUL

After we have been regenerated, we should not live and walk and do things by ourself anymore. As long as we live by ourself, we will be under the bondage of Satan. Perhaps you may say, "I don't think I live or do things by myself." Here is the need to discern the spirit from the soul; then you will see how much you are in the soul. You say that you are not living or doing things by yourself, but I would ask, By what are you living? By the flesh? Probably you will answer, "No, no, I am not living by the flesh!" Then, are you living by the spirit? You say, "Well, I doubt it." If you are neither living by the flesh nor by the spirit, by what are you living? The answer is that you are merely living by the soul. You say, "Oh, I don't like to commit any sin, I don't like to be fleshly, I don't like to cooperate with Satan. I love God. I like to follow the Lord and walk in the Lord's way. I like, I like, I like...." Still you are in the soul! Tell the Lord where you are. You yourself doubt very much that you are in the spirit. If you are not in the flesh nor in the spirit, you are in the soul. Praise the Lord, you are not in Egypt, for you have experienced the Passover. You have been delivered out of Egypt, but you have not yet entered into the good land of Canaan. You are still wandering in the wilderness of the soul.

(1) Human Love

Now we come to this issue: How can we discern the spirit from the soul? How can we know when we are in the spirit or in the soul and how can we divide the spirit from the soul? Look into the Word of the Lord.

"He that loveth father or mother more than me is not worthy of me; and he that loveth son or daughter more than me is not worthy of me. And he that doth not take his cross and follow after me, is not worthy of me. He that findeth his life shall lose it; and he that loseth his life for my sake shall find it" (Matt. 10:37-39).

"Life" here in the Greek text is the same word as that for "soul." The taking up of the cross in these verses refers to our human love for our dear ones. Human love is something in our soul, and it must be dealt with by the cross. How much do we love our dear ones? If we want to know how to discern the spirit and the soul, we should check our love. How do we love our parents, our children, our mother or father? How do we love our brother or sister? This is not man's word, but the Word of the Lord. Discernment of the spirit from the soul is only reached when we have checked our human and natural love. Our natural love has to be dealt with by the cross. In the New Testament Epistles the Holy Spirit tells us that husbands must love their wives, wives must submit to their husbands, parents must take care of their children, and children must honor and respect their parents. But all this must be in the resurrection-life. Natural affection, natural love, and natural relationships have to be cut off by the cross. After being dealt with by the cross, we will be in the spirit, which means that we will be in the resurrection-life. We will live in the resurrection-life—not in the natural life, but in the spiritual life. One test of how much our soul has been broken is how much the cross has dealt with our natural love and affection. When the natural love has been cut off by the cross, we will lose our soul.

Furthermore, if we are going to lose our soul by dealing with the natural love, we need to learn how to hate.

"If any man cometh unto me, and hateth not his own father, and mother, and wife, and children, and brethren, and
sisters, yea, and his own life also, he cannot be my disciple.
Whosoever doth not bear his own cross, and come after me,
cannot be my disciple" (Luke 14:26, 27).

"Life" here again in the Greek text is the same as that for
"soul." Besides the love for our dear ones, we also have self-love,
that is, the love for self or for our soul. The taking up of the
cross has much to do with this self-love. "If any man cometh
unto me, and *hateth* not...." Hateth whom? Our enemies? We
must love our enemies, but we must learn to hate our soul,
ourself. To hate ourself has something to do with the losing of
our soul. By hating ourself we can then cross out the self in our
soul.

(2) Love of the World

"And he said unto all, If any man would come after me,
let him deny himself, and take up his cross daily, and follow
me. For whosoever would save his life shall lose it; but whosoever shall lose his life for my sake, the same shall save it.
For what is a man profited, if he gain the whole world, and
lose or forfeit his own self?" (Luke 9:23-25).

"Remember Lot's wife. Whosoever shall seek to gain his
life shall lose it: but whosoever shall lose his life shall pre-
serve it" (Luke 17:32, 33).

In all of these verses, "life" again in the Greek text is the
same word as that for "soul." These passages show that the soul
is much involved with the love of the world. To give up the love
of the world and worldly things means that we have to deal
with our souls. When the soul is cut off, then the love of the
world is given up. Therefore, these two things, the love of
the world and the soul, are related to each other.

"Remember Lot's wife." This is a wife, not a husband! It is
the story of a wife who loved the worldly things. The Lord says
to be careful. If you love the world, you will lose your soul. If
we love the things of the world, we will lose our soul in the bad
sense, but if we give up the love of the world, we will lose our
soul in the good sense. Brothers and sisters, the love of the
world is a proof of where our soul is.

(3) Natural Life

"Verily, verily, I say unto you, Except a grain of wheat fall into the earth and die, it abideth by itself alone; but if it die, it beareth much fruit. He that loveth his life loseth it; and he that hateth his life in this world shall keep it unto life eternal" (John 12:24, 25).

Here "life" again means "soul." By reading and considering these two verses carefully and deeply, we will see that the soul has much to do with the natural life and the natural strength. Our natural life and strength have to be dealt with by losing the soul. When our natural life and strength are put to death, our soul will then be broken. How does one discern the spirit from the soul? Simply by taking the cross to the self-life and by putting ourselves under death. The soul is deceived, because it does not appear sinful. Therefore, we must always learn to check the soul by putting the cross on the self.

Suppose we are fellowshipping with a brother. How can we discern whether our fellowship is of the spirit or of the soul? By putting the cross on ourselves, we will clearly know whether we are in the spirit or in the soul. I should not say, "I am not doing something evil. I am doing something good when I fellowship with a brother." Fellowship is good, but such a fellowship may be entirely in the soul! When the cross is applied to ourselves, we will immediately be clear whether our fellowship is in the spirit or in the soul. Never check the soul or spirit by the discernment of *good* or *evil*. This kind of checking will only put us in darkness. There is no other way to check the soul and spirit but by the cross. The only way to determine whether we are in the soul or in the spirit is by checking whether we are now on the cross. Do I have any element of my own interest, or am I self-centered in my activities? Has the cross been put on my self-interest and self-centeredness? Check yourself in this way. All decisions and all activities must be checked by the cross, not by the standard of good and evil. In every subject of conversation, has the self been crossed out? Do not analyze by considering, "Am I in the spirit or am I in the soul? Let me consider for a moment to see how deep my feeling is. If it is not so deep, I must be in the soul. But if it seems to be deep, I might be in the spirit." If we analyze in this way, we will really be troubled. Simply by one check, we can be made very clear: Have we been put on the cross? In other words have we denied the self, taken up the cross, and followed the Lord in the spirit? When we deny the self by taking up the cross, the Lord Christ will have the full ground in us, and it will be easy to go along with Him.

The New Testament teaching gives some place to chastisement, but the cross occupies a much greater place. Many times God's chastisement works together with the cross. But do not wait for God's chastisement. All the time we must learn to take up the cross, since we know that we have been crucified with Christ. Day by day we must learn the lesson to deny the self, to take up the cross and not to give any ground to the soul. If we do this, we will actually be one with the Lord in the spirit, and the Lord will take the ground to possess us and to saturate us with Himself.

CHAPTER FOURTEEN

THE PRINCIPLE OF THE CROSS

Many Christians know something about the cross, but they are not clear about the *principle* of the cross. What is the principle of the cross? According to the Scripture, God has two creations in the universe: the first is called the old creation, and the second the new creation. The new creation came into being by putting the old one to an end and starting something new. Only by putting the old creation to an end could the new creation come into existence. It was by the work of the cross that the old creation was put to an end, and it was through the cross that the new creation began in resurrection.

THE ITEMS OF THE OLD CREATION

What are the constituents of the old creation? The first item in the old creation is the *angels* with the angelic life, and the second is *man* with the human life. These are two kinds of beings with two kinds of lives. The archangel, the head of the angels, became rebellious against God and became Satan, which means "the adversary of God." Satan not only rebelled, but led the rebellion against God with a good number of angels following him. According to Revelation 12, one-third of the angels, the heavenly stars, followed Satan. These rebellious angels became the evil forces—the principalities, dominions, powers and authorities mentioned in Ephesians, chapters 1, 2, and 6. The rebellion of the angelic life produced the third and fourth items of the old creation: *Satan* and his *kingdom.*

Now let us briefly continue with the other items of the old creation. After the creation of the human life, the enemy of God also induced man to act against God. This act caused something to be injected into the human life, which was Sin—the singular, personified, and capitalized Sin. The very sinful nature and thought of Satan was injected into the human life. Sin in this universe was invented by the injection of the fallen angelic life into the human life. Sin was not created by God, but invented by the illegal union of the satanic life with the human life. So *Sin* is number five in the list of items in the old creation. And not only did singular Sin come into existence, but it also brought with it many sins. Therefore, the fruits of Sin, *sins,* are the sixth item on the list, including lying, murder, pride, fornication, etc. All these sins were produced from Sin.

The *world* is number seven. The world was not created by God. God created the earth, but Satan invented the world. Sin was invented in Genesis 3, but it was not until Genesis 4 that something was added to Sin, which was Satan's invented world. What is the world? The world is the system of all human life under Satan. The Greek word for world is "kosmos," which means a "system." God created man for Himself, but now Satan has systematized humanity. Man is no longer for God, but wholly systematized by Satan and for Satan.

Another item besides these in the old creation is *death,* which is the consequence of Sin and sins. The *flesh*—the transmuted body, poisoned and ruined by Satan—is also of the old creation. The body became flesh through the corruption of Satan as Sin. The *old man* is another item, which is nothing less than the whole man ruined by Satan. Man, who was originally created by God, is now ruined by Sin.

Next is the *self.* The soul was created by God, but has become the self, threatened and corrupted by the flesh. It is like the body. God originally created the body as a good and pure thing, but it was corrupted by Satan's sinful nature and became the flesh. The same principle applies to the soul, which was created pure and good, but later was influenced by the flesh. It was threatened and then controlled by the flesh, thereby becoming the self. Just as Sin corrupted the body and it became the flesh, so the flesh influenced and controlled the soul and it became the self.

Finally, the 12th item is the *whole creation*. The whole creation was damaged and corrupted by the rebellion of the angelic life and by the transgression of the human life. This brought the whole creation under a kind of groaning because of the bondage of corruption (Rom. 8).

THE CENTER OF THE OLD CREATION

These twelve items added together are the old creation. The old creation includes so many things. But we need to be clear at this point that fallen man became the very *center* of the old creation. He is related to each one of the twelve items of the old creation. First, Satan got into man and became one with him. Included with Satan is the kingdom of Satan; therefore, since Satan is in man, the kingdom of Satan is also in man. Satan is the prince of the world, so the world too is included in Satan and is also in man. And, of course, embodied in man are Sin and sins, which issue in death. The flesh, the old man, and the self are also in man; and man was, and still is, the head of all creation. (According to Genesis 1, man was ordained head of the whole creation.) Thus, man is related to the entire creation, and the whole creation is related to man and centralized in man. Man is the very center of the old creation in every aspect. He nearly becomes all-inclusive, but not in a good sense. If one would meet Satan, there is no need for him to go to some special place—by going to man he will meet Satan. If he desires to meet the kingdom of Satan, there is no need for him to go to the moon—by going to man he will meet the kingdom of Satan. It is the same with the world. Within man, as representing the old creation, there is Satan, the kingdom of Satan, the world, Sin, sins, death, flesh, the old man, etc. We are not a small man! On the contrary, we are a big, all-inclusive man in a bad sense. Now, the whole creation is centralized in man.

THE ENDING OF THE OLD CREATION

Praise the Lord, one day something happened: God Himself became incarnated in this man! This means that God put all creation upon Himself. When God put man upon Himself, He put all things of the old creation upon Himself. For

example, it says in the Scripture, that God made Christ to be
Sin—not plural sins, but singular "Sin" (2 Cor. 5:21). God has
also laid all our iniquities upon Christ (Isa. 53:6), who "bare
our sins in His body upon the tree" (1 Pet. 2:24). He was "in
the likeness of the flesh of sin" (Rom. 8:3): the likeness is the
likeness of the flesh, and this human flesh is the flesh of sin.
John 1:14 says that "the Word became flesh," that is, He
became a human person. When He became a human person
in flesh, He became a human person in a flesh of sin, since by
that time sin was within the human flesh. The flesh had
become the flesh of sin, and the Lord became incarnated in
this flesh. However, we must be careful, for if we say He
became the exact flesh that we have, that is, as far as our
sinful nature is concerned, we are wrong. Hence, Romans 8:3
tells us that He became just *the likeness* of the flesh of sin,
not the sinful nature of the flesh of sin.

In John 3:14, the Lord Jesus Himself told us that He was
typified by the brass serpent hanging on the pole, i.e., the
cross. The brass serpent had *only the likeness* of the serpent,
not the poisonous nature of the serpent. The Lord Jesus was
born of a virgin that He might have the likeness of the flesh
of sin, but He had nothing to do with man as far as the sinful
nature of the flesh was concerned. We must be very careful
about this matter. When the Lord was made sin, He was
made in the *likeness* of sin.

He not only put man upon Himself, but He also put Satan,
the kingdom of Satan, the world, Sin, sins, flesh, etc., upon
Himself. Here again we have to be careful. The Lord was
incarnated as a man, not as a serpent; but when He was crucified on the cross, He was crucified as a man in the form of
the serpent. Why? Because at this stage man was one with
Satan, the serpent. So the Lord Jesus and even John the Bap-
tist told the Pharisees that they were the seed of the serpent
and a generation of vipers. They were the seed of the serpent,
because they had the serpent's life; the poisonous nature of
the serpent was in them. In the eyes of God, they, as sinful
people, had become the serpent. But the Lord, incarnated as a
man, had only the likeness of the flesh of sin, not the sinful
nature that sinful people have. Like the brass serpent on the

pole, the Lord had only the likeness of the serpent, not the nature and the poison of the serpent.

Now we come to the cross. Christ first put on such a man, who was all-inclusive of the old creation, and then brought this man to the cross. There at the cross this all-inclusive man was crucified. This means *all things were put to an end. This is the principle of the Cross.* By this kind of death Christ brought man to the cross and thereby brought everything to an end. Not only was Christ crucified there, but so were man, the world, Satan and his kingdom, Sin, sins, the old man, etc. All things of the old creation were brought to an end by the cross of Christ. We must experience this all-inclusive death.

The following verses reveal the principle of the cross in putting all things of the old creation to an end:

1) The angelic life: Colossians 1:20;
2) The human life: Galatians 2:20;
3) Satan: Hebrews 2:14 and John 12:31;
4) The kingdom of Satan: Colossians 2:15 and John 12:31;
5) Sin: 2 Corinthians 5:21 and Romans 8:3;
6) Sins: 1 Peter 2:24 and Isaiah 53:6;
7) The world: Galatians 6:14 and John 12:31;
8) Death: Hebrews 2:14;
9) Flesh: Galatians 5:24;
10) The old man: Romans 6:6;
11) Self: Galatians 2:20;
12) All things, or creation: Colossians 1:20.

John 12:31 says that the world and the prince of this world, who is Satan, were to be judged and cast out. When did this happen? According to verse 24, it happened at the death of Christ on the cross. By His death, the world was judged and the prince of the world was cast out. Hebrews 2:14 declares that Christ took part in flesh and blood, that through death He might destroy, or annul, him that had the power of death, that is the devil. This verse reveals that Christ, by His death in flesh and blood, destroyed or annulled Satan, who had the power of death. Colossians 1:20 says He reconciled "all things" unto Himself. This proves that not only man was wrong with God, but all things were also wrong with God; otherwise, there would be no need for reconciliation. According to the context of this passage, all creation was dealt with by the cross.

We need to be deeply impressed with the kind of death that Christ died on the cross. That death was an all-inclusive death—this is why we must experience it. All that we have, all that we are, all that we do and all to which we are related have been brought to the cross. The cross is the *end of all things related to us*. Everything has been dealt with and already crucified on the cross. The cross is the only ground for all that we are and have. We have to put all things to the cross: our knowledge, our wisdom, our ability, etc. This is the principle of the cross. There is no other ground. We may think how "good" we are. The young people especially are always thinking how good they are: "We are young, we are good, we are not like the old folks...." No matter how good we are, we have to come to the cross. We have to be crucified and crossed out. The more good we are, the more we must be crossed out. Never be proud of being good. Regardless of whether we are good or evil, we all have to pass through the cross. We should not evaluate ourselves wrongly. There is but one evaluation; that is, we must put ourselves to death.

Nothing of the old creation is in the Church. The Church is the new man, the new creation. All things have passed away and everything has become new. This means that all things have been put to an end in death, and everything is new in resurrection. We have now seen the principle of the cross, and in the next chapter we will see the principle of the resurrection. We do trust that our minds will be open to see that all the things related to us, whether they be good or bad, must be utterly put to death. Then there will be the way for us to come into the resurrection and into the new creation.

Chapter Fifteen

THE PRINCIPLE OF RESURRECTION

In the last chapter we considered the twelve items of the old creation, the first of which was the angelic life. But here we need to point out that those angels who did not fall were not included in the old creation. Though at one time they were under the leadership of Satan, the former head of all the angels, they never followed him in his rebellion; therefore, they are separate from the old creation. Only the rebellious angels who followed Satan became a part of the old creation. Thus, the angelic life as the first of the twelve negative items of the old creation does not include those good angels. The fallen angels, after they rebelled, became the principalities, authorities, rulers and dominions in the heavenly places (Eph. 1, 2, 6; Col. 2). The wicked spirits, mentioned in Ephesians 6, are the fallen angels. The majority of the angels, who did not rebel, were not included in the old creation, which was brought to an end by Christ's crucifixion.

However, among the human race there is no such exception, for all humanity fell into the rebellion of the devil. The rebellion of the human race began with the first man, Adam, and includes every descendant of his. There are two groups of angels, those who never rebelled and those who rebelled, but as far as the human race is concerned there is only one group. The fallen human race is represented by Adam and is under the headship of Adam; so the whole human race through Adam is included in the fallen, old creation.

Indeed, Satan, the leader of the rebellious angels, is included in the old creation. Satan misused the authority given him and utilized it to form his kingdom (Matt. 12:26). According to Isaiah 14:12-14, Ezekiel 28:13, 14 and Luke 4:5-7, Satan was appointed by God in the very beginning as the head of the angels, and as such he received certain authority from God. The Lord Jesus in His temptation in the wilderness recognized the authority given to Satan. Under his rule, Satan formed a kingdom with a group of angels who also misused their power and authority.

After man was created, Satan came to induce man to sin; and with Sin in man, many fruits were produced, called sins. Following the fall, Satan then utilized all the necessities for man's existence—such as eating, clothing, marriage, housing, etc. These necessities had been created and ordained by God for man's existence, but Satan utilized them to systematize the whole human race. This satanic system is called the world.

Due to Sin, sins and the world, death came into the human race; and by the fall, Satan injected something of his own nature into the human body to corrupt it, causing it to be transmuted into flesh. Another result of the fall is that man as a whole was changed and became the old man. In addition, man's soul, under the threatening and influence of the flesh, became the self. The soul was originally created good, but through the fall the soul became the self.

Satan was the head of the angels, and Adam was the head of the rest of creation, but both representatives rebelled. Consequently, the whole creation was influenced and affected (Rom. 8:20-22 and Col. 1:20) and needed to be reconciled by Christ's redemption.

THE ALL-INCLUSIVE DEATH IN THE ETERNAL SPIRIT

All of these items compose the old creation, and, as we have seen, fallen man became the very center of it. All the negative things of the whole universe were gathered together and concentrated in man. Satan, with his kingdom and worldly system, was in man, along with Sin, sins, death, self, flesh, and the old man. Everything of the old creation, including all the negative things of the universe, was centralized in this fallen man.

Then Christ became incarnated as man. Christ put man upon Himself—not a small, simple man, but a man all-inclusive of the old creation. This is why Christ was incarnated as man, and as man was crucified on the cross in the form of a serpent. Before the cross Christ was a man, but on the cross He was a man *in the form* of a serpent. Moreover, Christ was made Sin on the cross (2 Cor. 5:21). When He was on the cross, God not only put all of our sins upon Him, but He also made Him Sin. God put all the iniquities and all the sins of the human race upon Christ, and at that time He also made Christ to be Sin in the form of Satan. Since all the negative things in the universe were concentrated and centralized in the fallen man, Christ came into this man and brought this man to the cross. When He brought this man to the cross, He brought every negative thing of the universe to the cross. When He put this man to an end, He also put the old creation to an end. All the twelve items of the old creation were terminated by the all-inclusive death of Christ on the cross. If we have the heavenly point of view and spiritual insight, we will jump up and say, "Hallelujah!"

The last chapters of Ezekiel show us the building of God's house, God's temple. If the whole picture were drawn on paper, one would discover that the altar, a type of the cross, is located exactly in the center of the whole construction. Both the vertical and horizontal measurements of the building pinpoint the altar at the center of God's temple. This is very interesting, for it portrays the all-inclusive death of Christ, which has brought the whole old creation to an end through the cross.

This all-inclusive death was accomplished by the *eternal Spirit*. We read in Hebrews 9:14: "...Christ...through the eternal Spirit offered himself without blemish unto God." The all-inclusive death of Christ occurred in the eternal Spirit. This term, the eternal Spirit, is mentioned only once in the Scriptures. When Christ was incarnated in man, He became the very center of the whole creation, which included all the negative things of the universe; and when Christ brought this fallen man to death upon the cross, He did it in the eternal Spirit. He ended this all-inclusive man in a Spirit that is eternal, One that has no beginning and One that can never be ended. In other words, the death of Christ ended everything but the eternal Spirit. Christ brought every negative thing with Him to the cross and ended it, but He remains the same because He is in the eternal Spirit. Though all things were ended on the cross,

His Spirit could never be ended. Therefore, it is by this Spirit that Christ was resurrected. Christ as a man brought all negative things to death. All things passed *into* death and were ended; only the eternal Spirit passed *through* death and remained. It was in this Spirit and by this Spirit that Christ was resurrected.

Romans 1:4 says that Christ was "...the Son of God with power, according to the spirit of holiness, by the resurrection from the dead." What does holiness mean? And why does it say the Spirit of holiness instead of the Holy Spirit? Holiness simply means separation. Even though this eternal Spirit went into death, He was and still is a Spirit of separation. Death could end everything else, but death could not end the eternal Spirit; He is different and separate from all things. He is the Spirit of holiness, proved by the resurrection from the dead. I may put some books and other items in the trash can to discard them, but if I put a man in the trash can, he will jump out! He will not be willing to be put to an end; he is different from the books. By jumping out, he separates himself from the other items; he becomes a man of separation. In like manner, all things went to the cross—man, Satan, everything—and were put to an end; but only the eternal Spirit, who also went to the cross and into death with Christ, could never be put to an end. He is the Spirit of separation. Death did everything it possibly could, but death could not hold this Spirit. It is by this different Spirit, this Spirit of separation, that Christ was resurrected.

THE REALITY OF RESURRECTION
IN THE ETERNAL SPIRIT

Romans 8:11 says: "But if the Spirit of him that raised up Jesus from the dead dwelleth in you, he that raised up Christ Jesus from the dead shall give life also to your mortal bodies through his Spirit that dwelleth in you." Who raised up Jesus from the dead? It is the same Spirit of separation. What Spirit shall quicken our mortal bodies? It is the Spirit of resurrection, who dwells in us. This means that the reality of resurrection and the principle of resurrection dwell in us. The principle of resurrection is the separation effected by this eternal Spirit, the One who could never be terminated by death.

Seeing that the principle of resurrection is in the eternal Spirit of separation, we must ask where this Spirit is today. We must say, "Hallelujah, He is in me!" Therefore, this principle of resurrection is also in us. May the Lord open our eyes to see the principle of the cross and the principle of resurrection—that is, everything was ended by death, and the eternal Spirit now dwells in us. If we see this, we will be transcendent. We will say, "Hallelujah!" There is no need for us to beg, to ask, to cry. We only need to say "Hallelujah" all the time.

John 11:25 tells us that Christ Himself is the resurrection. Martha, the sister of dead Lazarus, complained that the Lord came too late. It seemed to her that resurrection and life were a matter of time. If the Lord had come earlier, she reasoned, her brother would not have died. On the contrary, the Lord told her, in effect, that it was not a matter of time or space, but a matter of Christ. He said, "I AM the resurrection." Forget about time and space; *wherever Christ is* and *whenever Christ is,* there is always resurrection.

On the day of His resurrection when Christ came to His disciples, He breathed on them and said, "Receive ye the Holy Spirit." This very Spirit that they received included the principle and reality of His resurrection. Without this Spirit, the disciples could have nothing to do with His resurrection. Christ's resurrection is in this Spirit. If we have this Spirit, we have the reality of the resurrection; if we do not have this Spirit, we have nothing to do with the resurrection. The resurrection is simply Christ Himself, and the principle and reality of Christ's resurrection is the eternal Spirit, which can never be ended. This eternal Spirit, who is without beginning and without ending, is the very principle and the very reality of the resurrection. Anything else that is put to death will be ended; only the eternal Spirit can not be held or terminated by death. This is why, after the resurrection, Christ as resurrection came to His disciples and breathed on them, telling them to receive *His breath* as the eternal Spirit, the Spirit of separation. This very eternal Spirit, as the principle and reality of resurrection, came into the disciples, and this principle and this reality are now in us.

Two more verses will help us to understand this. In Philippians 1:19 Paul speaks of "the supply of the Spirit of Jesus Christ." It seems he said: "I am in prison, but I am not afraid, for within me there is the principle and the reality of resurrection. What is this resurrection within me? It is the Spirit of Jesus with bountiful, all-inclusive, all-sufficient supply." Then, in Philippians 3:10, he says, "That I may know him, and the power of his resurrection." What is the power of His resurrection? It is the supply of the Spirit of Jesus. The bountiful, all-inclusive, all-sufficient supply of the Spirit of Jesus is the power of His resurrection. This power and this supply are nothing less than the eternal Spirit, the Spirit of separation. Yet this Spirit is within us today! Isn't this enough? What more could we want? We should say, "Hallelujah!" We have to thank Him for His cross, and we have to praise Him also for His Spirit. His cross has ended everything negative, and now His eternal Spirit is indwelling us as the power of resurrection.

To summarize, we can never have a real experience of the cross unless we are in the eternal Spirit. No matter how much we know it and how much we talk about it, if we are not in the eternal Spirit, we can never experience the power of the cross. The more we live and walk in the eternal Spirit of separation, the more we will realize the killing power of the cross. There is no further need to reckon ourselves dead; this is committing spiritual suicide. Although many Christians try to commit spiritual suicide daily, yet, praise the Lord, they can never succeed! If we just live and walk in the Spirit, the all-inclusive dose within us, we will experience the killing power of the cross. Since the principle and reality of both His resurrection and His death are in the eternal Spirit, then the resurrection also *includes* the effectiveness of His death. In the eternal Spirit of resurrection there is the killing factor, the killing power of the cross.

So, again we say, Praise the Lord! As long as we are in the all-inclusive Spirit, the experience of the cross is ours and the reality of the resurrection is within us. There is no need to do anything but take it by living faith. If we see this, we will say, "Hallelujah, praise the Lord!" We have the living faith, and we take it and claim it by faith. Then the principles of the cross and of the resurrection will be real to us in the indwelling Spirit. We already have Him within. There is no need for us to ask anymore, but just to take Him and experience Him and enjoy Him. Then we will experience a real growth in life. I can assure you of this. This is a vision which we need to see and take by faith.

CHAPTER SIXTEEN

THE RICHES OF RESURRECTION

"For this is the covenant that I will make with the house of Israel after those days, saith the Lord; I will put my laws into their mind, and on their heart also will I write them: and I will be to them a God, and they shall be to me a people: and they shall not teach every man his fellow-citizen, and every man his brother, saying, Know the Lord: for all shall know me, from the least to the greatest of them" (Heb. 8:10, 11).

"And as for you, the anointing which ye received of him abideth in you, and ye need not that any one teach you; but as his anointing teacheth you concerning all things, and is true, and is no lie, and even as it taught you, ye abide in him" (1 John 2:27).

Both Hebrews 8 and 1 John 2 declare that today, under the New Testament, there is no need of any outward, human teaching. Hebrews 8:10 says that the law is written within us; thus, there is no need for any brother to teach us to know the Lord. First John 2:27 says that the *anointing* is abiding in us, so there is no need of any human teaching. One passage says that the "law" is written in us, and the other that the "anointing" is abiding in us. What are these two things? It is quite possible for us to be Christians for years and yet not know that we have these two wonderful things within us. We have a wonderful law written in us and a mysterious anointing abiding in us. How marvelous and yet pitiful if we do not realize it! It is due to the inner law and the inner anointing that we do not need any outward, human teachings.

THE CROSS AND RESURRECTION

The inner law and the inner anointing are something of the resurrection. We have seen the principle of the cross—that is, the all-inclusive ending of the negative things in the universe—and we have also seen the principle and the reality of the resurrection. The cross ends the old creation, whereas the resurrection produces the riches of the new creation. Through the cross the old creation is finished. By the Lord's death all twelve items of the old creation have been brought to the cross and completely crossed out. But that is not the end of the story, for after death came resurrection. What was resurrected? Satan? The kingdom of Satan? Sin? The flesh? A thousand times no! The eternal Spirit resurrected only the essence of what God originally created for His purpose.

The human nature was a part of God's original creation. God created the human nature for His purpose, but Satan damaged it. Therefore, by His death, the Lord brought the Satan-damaged nature into death; but by His resurrection, the Lord brought the God-created nature into resurrection. The Lord not only redeemed the human nature, but uplifted this human nature to a higher standard. So the new creation consists of Christ in the eternal Spirit and the recovered and uplifted human nature in resurrection.

What are the items of the riches of resurrection? First, there is the Triune God, not in the sense of the Old Testament, but in the New Testament sense. Then there is the divine, eternal life, which is God Himself as our life. (The difference between God and divine life is the same as that between electricity and light. Strictly speaking, electricity is the light, and the light is the electricity, but there is still a distinction. For example, the electricity is used not only as light, but also as power and heat, etc. Similarly, God Himself is our life as well as many other things.) The third item is the divine nature (2 Pet. 1:4). The fourth, the law of life (Rom. 8:2; Heb. 8:10). The fifth, the anointing (1 John 2:27). These five items are the all-inclusive riches of resurrection—all other things that one may name are included in these. The new creation inherits all these items in the resurrection.

All the riches of resurrection, we can say, are simply God Himself. The divine nature is certainly God Himself, and the law of life and the anointing are also something of God Himself and His moving. Man, however, is not one of the riches of resurrection, but one who is recovered and uplifted by these riches. We are somewhat familiar with the Triune God, the divine life, and the divine nature, but most Christians are not familiar with the law of life and the inner anointing. In today's Christianity these have been neglected. But the inner law and the inner anointing are the practical riches of resurrection—if we do not know them, we cannot know the resurrection in a practical way. The resurrection will only be known objectively unless we know the law of life and the inner anointing; only thus can we experience the resurrection in a subjective way.

THE LAW AND THE PROPHETS

Let us consider the Old Testament with the law and the prophets. In a sense the Old Testament was even called the law and the prophets (Matt. 7:12; 22:40). What is the difference between the two? The law is a set of fixed rules which cannot be changed. For instance, one item of the law requires everyone to honor his parents. This is a changeless rule, and everyone must keep it. There is no need to seek guidance about honoring one's parents; this law is fixed. Another rule is, "Thou shalt not steal." It is also an established, fixed rule. There is no need to pray: "Lord, tell me whether or not it is Your mind to steal. Give me guidance about stealing." There is no need to seek such guidance. This same principle applies to the rest of the ten commandments. Thus, the law is a set of fixed rules which everyone must keep. It does not alter with each individual. Regardless of whether a person is a man or a woman, old or young, rich or poor, he is compelled to keep the rules.

Now what about the prophets? The prophets speak to the individual situation. Suppose someone came to Jeremiah and asked, "Is it all right for me to go to Jerusalem?" The prophet might say this time, "You may go." But another time he might say, "You may not." The prophets give the living guidance of the Lord according to the different individual situations. The law has no changes, but the prophets have many changes depending upon the situation of those involved. Once we have the law, we always have it, for the commandments are permanent; whereas the guidance from the prophets only holds for the occasion. The prophet, therefore, must be contacted continuously. The one who sought Jeremiah could not say, "One month ago, the prophet said it was all right for me to go Jerusalem; therefore, I can go now without consulting him." If he desired to go to Jerusalem again, he must seek guidance from the prophet once more. Whether or not he should honor his parents requires no guidance, for this is a fixed principle of the law; but *how* to honor his parents is definitely a matter of guidance. Should he honor his parents on a certain occasion by this way, or by that way? Guidance is needed; therefore, he must contact the prophet.

The Old Testament forbids women to wear men's clothing and men to wear women's clothing. This was clearly established by the Lord as a settled rule and a changeless law. But when we are shopping for an article of clothing, one item may be worth $200 and another $20. This becomes a matter for seeking the Lord's guidance, not His law. This is the difference between the law and the prophets. The fixed principle of the law varies with no one, but the guidance of the prophets varies with all. Sometimes with even the same person it may vary from one occasion to another.

THE INNER LAW AND THE INNER ANOINTING

Is there then any law in the New Testament? There is, but it is not the law of letters. In the New Testament there is only the law of life. This is not an outward law, but an inward law; not the law written on tablets of stone, but the law written on the heart. What about prophets in the New Testament? As the law of life replaces the law of letters, so the inner anointing succeeds the prophets. For example, if I were to have my hair cut, should I seek the Lord's guidance by praying, "Lord, show me if I should have my hair cut like a cowboy, or like a movie star"? There is no need to seek guidance in matters such as this, for there is a law within me forbidding a movie-star or cowboy style of haircut. The inner law of life regulates me in such matters. Suppose you are a sister in the Lord, and you try to have your hair styled like the movie stars. Something deep within will regulate and check you. This is the inner regulating of the law of life. In more than a thousand chapters of the Scriptures there is not one word prohibiting stylish hairdos like the movie stars. The movie stars are not even mentioned in the Scriptures! But there is an inner law regulating you from patterning yourself after the movie stars.

Suppose a brother is about to minister the Word of the Lord. There is no need for him to ask, "Lord, should I wear cowboy pants?" If he proceeds to dress this way, the inner regulating law will check and prohibit him. This is a fixed principle of the law within him. Neither is there any need for him to seek guidance about cutting his hair like the cowboys. But *when* and *where* to get his hair cut is a matter of the Lord's guidance. Therefore, he has to pray, "Lord, is it Thy will for me to get my hair cut today? Should I get it cut in the barber shop or in the home of a brother?" This is not a matter of the inner law, but of the inner anointing. The anointing within is his indwelling "Prophet," who gives him guidance. If he becomes careless and does not seek the guidance of the "the Prophet" within, he may go hastily to a brother to get his hair cut and have some trouble. Due to his carelessness about the anointing within he must suffer. Do you see the point?

Most of the ladies like to buy things! When they enter the department store, they have no limitation and no regulation except that of their checking account. But the dear sisters who love the Lord and learn to live and walk by the Lord have a different story. When they enter the department store and pick up an item, there is something within regulating them and saying, "Drop it." And they drop it. When they pick up another item, again, "Don't touch it; drop it." What is this inner protest? This is the inner law, the law of life. The worldly ladies can pick up anything they desire, regardless of design, color, and shape. If they like it, they buy it. But the sisters who love the Lord have an inner negative feeling when they pick up this item or that. This is the regulating of the inner law.

On the other hand, if you need to purchase a certain item, you have to seek the guidance of the inner anointing as to how much you should spend for it. You need to fellowship with the Lord, seeking His guidance through the inner anointing. No one else can tell you. If you brought the problem to me I would say, "Don't ask me; ask the Inner One. You know how much you should spend by the anointing within you." Just say, "Lord, $150?" The inner anointing may say, "No." "$95?" "No." "$65?" "Maybe." "$50?" "O.K.!" Something within you will feel "O.K."

The husband cannot even tell his wife what she should do. If the wife asks her husband about a $30 hat, he had better say, "Dear, you must go to the Lord and seek His guidance by the inner anointing." The inner anointing will tell her, but she needs time to pray and contact the Lord. "Lord, I worship You. You are my Life! You are my Lord! and You are dwelling within me. Lord, give me the proper feeling as to how much to spend for a hat." Then she will sense the Lord inside: "$30?" "No." "$25?" "No." "$20?" "No." "$15?" "No." "$12?" "O.K." Finally, the inner anointing will give her a proper inner sense.

If you do not have this kind of experience, I am afraid you may not be a child of God. "As many as are *led* by the Spirit of God, these are sons of God" (Rom. 8:14). How does the Spirit of God lead us? By the inner anointing. Praise the Lord, we are the new creation in the resurrection. In the resurrection we have the Triune God Himself, we have Him as our life and as our nature, and we also have both the inner law of life and His Spirit working within us as the ointment, continually moving and anointing us with God Himself. The more we are anointed by this practical way, the more we will have the very essence of God within us. It is just like a painter, painting a table. The more he paints the table, the more paint is added to it. The more we have the anointing of the Holy Spirit within us, the more we will gain the substance of God Himself. If we are willing to be continually anointed by the Holy Spirit within us, after a certain period of time we will have more of God's essence or substance. God Himself is the paint, the Holy Spirit is the painter and the anointing is the painting. The Holy Spirit is painting us inwardly with God Himself as the paint. This painting will give us the inner sense of the Lord's will.

We must have the inner regulating and the inner anointing. We are regulated by the inner law to be kept in the Lord's way, and we are anointed by the inner anointing to know the Lord's will in everything. In this way the very essence of God Himself is increased within us all the time. The more we are painted by the Holy Spirit with God as the paint, the more the substance of God Himself will be added within us. These are the riches of the resurrection as our inward, practical experience.

CHAPTER SEVENTEEN

THE FELLOWSHIP
OF LIFE AND THE SENSE OF LIFE

"That which was from the beginning, that which we have heard, that which we have seen with our eyes, that which we beheld, and our hands handled, concerning the Word of life (and the life was manifested, and we have seen, and bear witness, and declare unto you the life, the eternal life, which was with the Father, and was manifested unto us); that which we have seen and heard declare we unto you also, that ye also may have fellowship with us: yea, and our fellowship is with the Father, and with his Son Jesus Christ: and these things we write, that our joy may be made full. And this is the message which we have heard from him and announce unto you, that God is light, and in him is no darkness at all. If we say that we have fellowship with him and walk in the darkness, we lie, and do not the truth: but if we walk in the light, as he is in the light, we have fellowship one with another, and the blood of Jesus his Son cleanseth us from all sin" (1 John 1:1-7).

In this short passage there is first the eternal life. From this eternal life is the divine fellowship, and this divine fellowship brings in the light which is God Himself. So here is the life, the fellowship, and the light.

Romans 8:6 tells us, "To set the mind on the flesh is death, but to set the mind on the spirit is life and peace" (R.S.V.). This verse speaks of death as well as life and peace. We must realize that either death or life and peace, as mentioned here, are something we can sense deeply within us. Otherwise, how could we know that we have this death or that we have the life and peace? We know that we have death or life and peace by the sense within us. The word "sense" does not occur in this verse, but it is clear that when we set our mind on the flesh we know death by sensing it, and, on the other hand, when we set our mind upon the spirit we know life and peace also by sensing them. Therefore, there is the inner sense of life in this verse. It appears that this verse has nothing to do with 1 John, but in the reality of the spirit it is very much related to the first chapter of 1 John. In 1 John, chapter one, there is the fellowship of life, and in Romans 8:6 there is the sense of life.

In the last chapter we have seen that the law of life and the anointing are among the riches of resurrection. We also have God Himself, the divine life, which is Christ in the Spirit, and the divine nature as our riches. These are the five main items of the riches in resurrection, and as those in the new creation we have the position and full right to enjoy them. Upon the ground of the new creation we can experience the resurrection, which includes God as our portion, Christ as our life, the divine nature, the law of life, and the inner anointing. Consider how rich these things are! Day by day we are enjoying these five items of riches in the resurrection, whether we realize it or not. Even as a new-born child of God, we enjoy these riches and live by these riches every day.

THE FELLOWSHIP OF LIFE

From the riches of God Himself, the divine life, the divine nature, the law of life and the inner anointing, there are two other items: the fellowship of life and the sense of life. These are the products of the riches of resurrection. The eternal life brings a divine fellowship. When we have Christ as life in the Spirit, we have fellowship with that life. The fellowship of life is just like the current of blood. The blood in our body is the life of our body—if our body contains no blood, there is no life, for the life is in the blood. There is also the current of blood in the body, and through the current of blood all the negative elements are eliminated from the body and nourishment is transmitted to every part of the body. Day by day the current of blood is bearing away the waste products and carrying the supply of nourishment to every member of the body. The current of blood continually fulfills these two functions.

Negatively, it washes the members of the body and carries away the refuse, and positively, it supplies health to the body.

What, then, is the fellowship of life? As the blood is the life, so our spiritual blood is Christ in the Spirit as our life. With Christ, our spiritual blood, as our life there is the current of life. Christ as our life is flowing within us all the time just as the current of blood is continually flowing in the body, and this flowing of life is the fellowship of life. It is by this flowing of life, this fellowship of life, that all the riches of Christ are carried to us. The continual flowing of the riches of Christ meets our need of nourishment on the positive side and of cleansing and discharge on the negative side. Only the medical profession can tell us how much nourishment and discharge has been daily effected by the current of blood. Thus, the fellowship of life is the flowing current of the eternal life, which is Christ.

Consider the light bulb, for instance. The current of electricity to the bulb is registered at the meter. If the current is stopped at the meter, no light will appear in the bulb. All the functions of electricity depend on the current of electricity. When the current of electricity is turned off, the function of the bulb to give light ceases.

Before we as unbelievers were saved, we did not have this flowing current. I remember my own experience very well. Before I was saved, I did not have the living feeling flowing within me. But since I was saved, the more I have loved the Lord, contacted Him and lived for Him, the more I have sensed something within me flowing and flowing and flowing. This is the current of life or the fellowship of life. The eternal life, which is the Son of God, is so real and substantial. It can even be heard and seen, touched and handled, declared and preached (1 John 1:1-3). Since we have received this life, we have the fellowship, the current, of life. Through this fellowship of life it is very easy for us to be brought into the presence of God.

THE SENSE OF LIFE

How can we know when we are in the presence of God? God is light, and when we are in the presence of God, we can sense the light. Not only do we sense the inner flowing, but also the inner shining which comes only through the fellowship of life. This is not a doctrine, but an explanation of our experience. If we cannot say "amen" to these experiences, then I am afraid there is something wrong with us. This is exactly what we should have experienced since the day of our salvation, although we may not have been able to explain it. Allow me to repeat: something within us is moving and flowing, and when we are in the flow, we are simply in the presence of God. Then we have the shining within us, and everything is in the light. We are clear about all things— whether this is right or wrong, whether this is the will of God or not, whether this is something of death or of life. All things are made clear by the inner sense.

The sense of life, therefore, is very much related to the fellowship of life. The fellowship of life helps us to realize the sense of life by bringing us into the presence of God, where we may enjoy the shining of God as light. This shining makes us clear about everything. It penetrates into every corner and avenue of our being, bringing to us a very tender and keen sense. A slight mistake is immediately detected by this sense. The more we have the flowing of life, the more we are in the presence of God, and the more shining we will experience. The more we experience this shining, the more we will realize a keen and tender sense. It is by this sense that we can know God, His will, and His way. This sense searches and tests everything.

Furthermore, this inward sense of life always depends upon the degree of our inward relationship with the Lord. When we set our mind on the flesh, as we have pointed out in Romans 8:6, we are simply setting the self on the flesh. To set the mind on the flesh means that our self is cooperating with the flesh, and if we cooperate with the flesh, our relationship with God, of course, is wrong. Remember the three concentric circles illustrating the three parts of man. The flesh is the body (outer circle) changed in nature through Satan's corruption. The mind is in the soul (middle circle), representing our human being, the self. The Triune God dwells in the spirit (center circle). The mind, located between the flesh and the spirit, has the possibility of moving in either direction. Never forget Romans 8:6—it is one of the most important verses in the Scriptures. In a sense it is even more important than John 3:16. If we only remember John 3:16 and forget Romans 8:6, we are a poorly saved Christian; we could never be a victorious Christian. John 3:16 is adequate for us to receive eternal life, but Romans 8:6 points out how to be a victorious Christian.

To set our mind—that is, to set our self—upon the flesh is death. To set our mind, or our self, upon the spirit is life and peace. Here is the key to death or life. The mind is quite neutral: it is on the fence. It may turn toward the flesh, or it may turn toward the spirit. Again, the story of the garden of Eden must be repeated. The free will can make either of two choices. To choose the tree of knowledge means death, but to choose the tree of life means life. We are between these two; we are neutral to life and death. The issue depends on our choice, our attitude. Personified Sin, representing Satan, is in the flesh; the Triune God is in the spirit after we are saved; and the self is in the mind. The secret of life or death is dependent upon our cooperating with the spirit or with the flesh. When we cooperate with the flesh, we have death; when we cooperate with the spirit, we are partakers of God, who is life.

(1) Sensing the Taste of Death

How do we know that we have death? We know by sensing it. Death gives us a certain kind of inward sense. One such sense is that of *emptiness*. We sense death when we feel empty within. Another sense death gives us is a sense of *darkness*. When we sense darkness within us, we have death. Death also gives us the feeling of *uneasiness*, which includes restlessness and disturbance. This is a sense of nothing soothing within us, a sense of everything within being in a state of friction—no peace, no rest, no comfort, no calm. Another sense of death is *weakness*. Often we say, "I cannot bear it any longer." This indicates that we are so weak. We have no strength, no force, no weight to stand against our frustrations. Finally, death gives us the sense of *depression, oppression,* or *suppression*—all these

"-pressions"! Because we are weak, it is easy for us to be depressed. Why? Because our mind is set upon the flesh, which results in death. Emptiness, darkness, uneasiness, weakness, and depression—all these are the tastes of the sense of death. We know death within when we sense the emptiness, the darkness, the uneasiness, the weakness, and the depression. This kind of sense proves that we are in the flesh and standing with the flesh.

But this sense of death really comes from the sense of life. Suppose a person is truly dead, a corpse. He would not have any sense of emptiness, darkness, uneasiness, and so forth, because he does not have life. But if he has life within, though the life may be sickly and weak, he still has a certain sense of emptiness and darkness. He is able to sense all these things, because he is still a living person. As a living person, he is contacting death, and it is the life within him that gives him the death sense. One of the functions and purposes of the sense of life is to sense the taste of death.

(2) Sensing the Taste of Life and Peace

The sense of death, however, is only something negative. On the positive side is the sense of life and peace. What is the sense, the taste, of life and peace? First of all, in contrast with emptiness, there is *satisfaction* and fullness. We sense that we are satisfied with the Lord. We are full in His presence, neither thirsty nor hungry. Secondly, we sense *light,* the opposite of darkness. Along with our inward satisfaction we have the light shining within us. Every corner and every avenue of our being is full of light. Every part is transparent; nothing is opaque. Then, in contrast to uneasiness, we have *peace,* which soothes all our disturbances. Peace with rest, peace with comfort, peace with ease is the sense within us. There is no feeling of friction or controversy. *Strength* versus weakness is another taste of the sense of life. We feel the full strength and power of life. There is a living dynamo within us; and it seems as if there is not only one, but four motors. Sometimes we feel the horsepower of a million horses. Oh, there is a real strengthening within us that overcomes all our weakness! We do not care about the long faces of our wives. If our wives jump on us, we will say,

"Hallelujah!" They will not upset us and cause us to lose our temper, for we are strong. We are not light and weak; we are weighty and full of power. Nothing can turn us upsidedown! Praise the Lord! This is the inner sense of life and peace. Finally, in contrast with depression we have *liberty*. Through the flowing of life we are not only liberated, but also transcendent above all oppression. Nothing can suppress us. The more the depression comes, the more we are in the heavenlies.

This is how we perceive life and peace. We simply perceive them by sensing them, and we sense them because we have life. This life within us is a flowing life. Through the flowing of life we are living and in the presence of God. Therefore, we have the deep, inward sense that we are satisfied, enlightened, strengthened, comforted, uplifted, liberated, and transcendent! The more we are in the fellowship of life, the more we will sense the life; and the more we sense life, the more we will enjoy the increased fellowship of life. These two are always experienced in cycles—that is, the more fellowship of life, the more sense of life; the more sense of life, the more fellowship of life. This is wonderful! Praise the Lord!

The fellowship and sense of life are by-products of the resurrection. The main riches of the resurrection are God Himself, Christ as life, the divine nature, the law of life, and the anointing of the Holy Spirit. From these riches issue the secondary, but practical things: the fellowship of life and the sense of life.

CHAPTER EIGHTEEN

THE EXERCISE OF AND ENTRANCE INTO THE SPIRIT

In chapter seventeen we have seen that the divine life which we have received issues in the fellowship of life, or the current of life, and this current of life produces the inner feeling, the deeper consciousness of life. Now let us consider the difference between the soul and the spirit.

Bear in mind that the tabernacle, or the temple, has three parts: the outer court, the holy place, and the Holiest of all. Remember that the New Testament definitely declares that we are the temple of God. Therefore, the tabernacle, or the temple, is not only the type of Christ, but also of Christians. The human being consists of three parts: the body, the soul, and the spirit (1 Thes. 5:23). These three parts correspond with the three parts of the tabernacle: the body with the outer court, the soul with the holy place, and the spirit with the Holiest of all.

In the type of the tabernacle, God's presence or the Shekinah glory of God and the ark, which was the type of Christ, were in the Holiest of all. Christ in our spirit is the New Testament application or fulfillment of this type. Today, He is in the inmost part of our being, which is now the Holiest of all.

This is why the book of Hebrews deals with this matter. Chapter 4, verse 12, as we have seen, sets forth the need to divide the spirit from the soul. In other words, we need to discern the spirit from the soul in order to realize in our experience the living Christ, who dwells in our spirit. This conforms with the teachings of the whole New Testament. The four Gospels exhort us to deny and renounce the soul, and the Epistles encourage us to walk after the spirit and live in the human spirit. It is in this spirit that the Lord Jesus as the divine Spirit dwells (2 Tim. 4:22). Therefore, we discern the human spirit from the soul by denying the soul and by following the Lord in our spirit.

THE EXPERIENCE OF THE ALTAR

Let us consider a problem in the application of this principle. A sister once came to me saying: "If we are not in the Holiest of all, it means that we are still in the body or the soul. How, then, could we exercise the spirit?" It seems quite logical. If we are still in the body or the soul and have not entered into the spirit, how could we exercise the spirit? We cannot answer this question by any mental process. However, when we are still living in the body or the soul, it does not mean that we are wholly cut off from the spirit. When we exercise our hands or our feet, does that mean our hands or our feet are cut off from the head? We are a whole being: body, soul, and spirit. We cannot cut this being into three parts. I told this sister that even when she repented and believed on the Lord Jesus, her repentance was an exercise of the spirit. Real repentance requires a contrite spirit. If repentance is merely in our mentality, it is not a deep and real repentance. It must be realized deeply within our spirit. When we received the Lord Jesus, we exercised our spirit, though we had no conscious knowledge of the term *spirit*. Every stage in our experience of the Lord is something in our spirit.

When we received the Lord Jesus as our Savior, we came to the cross, where we were redeemed. In the type of the tabernacle the cross was typified by the altar which was located in the outer court. We repented and received the Lord Jesus at the cross. At the very moment we were saved, there was a real exercise of our spirit. Because we exercised our spirit, we touched God, sensed God, and had a living contact with God.

But perhaps afterwards, we did not live by the spirit or even by the soul, but by the ways of the world. Yes, we were saved at the cross, which meant we passed by the altar in the outer court; but we did not subsequently live by the spirit, nor even by the soul, but according to the worldly ways.

You may ask what are the worldly ways. Let me illustrate by telling about a brother by the name of Sun, who originally was a judge in a law court. One day he was brought to the gospel meeting, where I was preaching. After the meeting, this unbeliever came to me with a worldly question: "Oh, Mr. Lee, please tell me, is God a male or a female?" Well, I just told him a little bit about God and Christ. Then he said that he was really "impressed" by my preaching, but he did not know how to believe. I told him simply to open himself to receive Christ, for Christ is a Spirit and He is everywhere. I said, "Go home and close your door; kneel down, confess your sins, and open yourself to Christ. Tell Him that you believe He died for you, and that you receive Him as your Savior." He promised that he would do it.

That night while with his family, who knew nothing about Christianity, he suddenly closed the door to his room. His wife and son asked him what he was going to do, to which he replied that he had some special business, and that he had to close the door. He knelt down and prayed. His wife and son, spying through the window, wondered why he was kneeling down and laughed at him. After he prayed, he thought something would suddenly happen to him, but nothing did. The next morning after breakfast he had to go to court to take care of a case, and on his way, all of the sudden, something happened. He told me the whole universe changed. How wonderful the heaven and the earth were! Even the little dog and cat, which he formerly despised, were now so pleasant to him. He was so joyful that he began to laugh. He wondered, "What is this?" When he entered the court and began his case, he could not control his laughing; and after the case, he came home laughing more and more. His wife asked, "What happened to you? Did you get a lot of money? What makes you so happy and joyful?" He replied, "I don't know. I am simply joyful! Everything in the universe is changed." The next day he met a young brother who helped him to realize that he was really saved.

Afterward, however, although he was saved, he continued to act and live in a worldly way and look at things as worldly people look at them. He was still in the outer court under the sun; all his senses were the same as before. On the third day he was brought again to the church meeting. I was happy to see him there. After the meeting he said, "Mr. Lee, you are a good speaker and quite eloquent. From what school did you graduate?" His remarks revealed the worldly way he looked at things. Then he conversed with me about many matters concerning the church. He said, "How did you bring in so many people? What means did you use? Did you advertise or use some kind of propaganda like a political party?" This is a totally worldly way of looking at things. Then he asked me, "Mr. Lee, I would like to be a Christian. Please tell me the procedure. Do I have to fill out some forms or sign some papers?" Of course, I helped him to have the right understanding. But then he asked me, "Suppose I become a member of your church, how much money do I have to contribute yearly? And what shall I do with my family? Will your church control my whole family? Will you give many regulations to my wife and child?" What is this? This is the worldly way. This person was really saved, but all these things proved that he was still in the outer court, still in Egypt. He experienced the Passover, but he had not yet crossed the Red Sea. He was still in the physical world.

THE EXPERIENCE OF THE FIRST VEIL

Let us continue to use this brother as an illustration. He was saved in 1938. The next year, nothing happened. He was really saved, but he was still entirely in the world. For three years nothing happened. Then in 1941, he was revived; something revolutionized him. One day, while praying, he dropped everything worldly. He said, "Lord, I give up my knowledge, my job as a judge, my family, and everything of the world. Oh, Lord, from now on I love Thee! I was saved three years ago; but now I know I have to drop everything worldly." He gave up the world.

In so doing, this brother passed through the first veil from the outer court and entered into the holy place. From that very day, he discovered how to fellowship with Christ and how to take Christ as his daily manna through the reading of his Bible. His Bible became very precious and sweet to him. Every day he enjoyed taking something from the Bible as food. Since that day he not only enjoyed the showbread on the table, but was also enlightened by the light within. Then, too, he had the joy of praying. He told me, "Oh, Brother Lee (he never called me Mr. Lee anymore), whenever I close my eyes and pray, I just have the feeling that I am in the heavens." What is this? It is the sweet savor of the burnt incense. He felt the presence of God, because he had the experience of Christ as his daily manna, as the inner light and as the sweet savor of resurrection.

At this point we need to be very clear as to where this was experienced. He entered from the outer court to the holy place by passing through the first veil. He did not pass through the second veil. First, his sins were dealt with at the altar of the cross; but the world and the worldly things were still upon him. Three years later, by passing through the first veil, he dropped the world and the worldly things and entered into the holy place. Day by day he started to experience Christ as his life, as his food, as his light, and as his sweet savor of resurrection.

THE EXPERIENCE OF THE SECOND VEIL

But still he was not in the Holiest of all. The sins and the worldly things were gone, but one thing remained—the flesh. Hence, there was still another veil of separation. Through recent correspondence from the Far East, I learned that this brother, during the last year or two, has been experiencing the breaking of the outer man. The breaking of the outer man is the rending of the second veil! It is the rending or breaking of the flesh. The letters reveal that from this experience, he is receiving the real discernment of the spirit. He can not only discern his own spirit, but also the spirit of others, because now he is more in the spirit.

When we entered the outer court through salvation, our sins were dealt with. When we entered the holy place, the world was put to death. The self, however, is still left if we have not entered the Holiest of all. Day by day we can enjoy Christ as the wonderful manna, as the heavenly light, and as the sweet savor of resurrection; but this is still rather shallow, for everything in the holy place is openly displayed. The show-bread is not the *hidden* manna, the light is not the *hidden* law, and the incense is not the *hidden* rod of resurrection. When we come into the meeting, everyone can see that we are show-ing the manna, shining the light and spreading the sweet odor of the burnt incense. If this is the case, we should not think that we are so deep. Many times when we come to the meet-ing with the sweet odor of the burnt incense, some would comment: "Oh, what a nice brother! Such a sweet sister! Whenever they open their mouth, everyone senses the sweet savor of Christ."

But this is not the hidden manna, the hidden law, and the hidden, budded rod. However, these good experiences of the holy place should not be rejected. On the contrary, we should respect them. Praise the Lord, many are enjoy-ing Christ as their daily manna. Day by day they are also enjoying Christ as their light and as their sweet savor in res-urrection. But we must realize that this is not the goal; this is not the land of Canaan. This is only the wilderness, where there is the living Rock flowing with the living water and where Christ is supplying us with the daily manna. To par-take of the manna from heaven and the living water flowing out of the Rock does not prove that we are in the goal of God. It only proves that we are not in Egypt, that is, not in the world. In other words we are in the holy place, but not in the Holiest of all. It is holy, but it is not the holiest. We must press on to enjoy the best. It is not good enough to be merely out of Egypt—this is only the negative aspect. There is some-thing much more positive. We need to enter into the good land which is the type of the all-inclusive Christ in our spirit. Nei-ther the Passover Lamb in Egypt, nor the daily manna in the wilderness can compare with the good land of Canaan. The good land of Canaan includes not just one aspect or one part of Christ, but the all-inclusive Christ.

Again, we must point out that when we were saved, unconsciously we exercised our spirit. There is no doubt about this. Now in the holy place, day by day we read the Scriptures, contact Christ, and experience the shining of the light. All of this must also be experienced by exercising our spirit, even though we may be a person in the soul rather than in the spirit. Perhaps we read the Scriptures in the morning by exercising our spirit and thereby feed on Christ as our daily manna. But as far as we ourselves are concerned, we are not yet in the spirit; we are still in the soul. Finally, one day we will realize that the self must be dealt with and broken. When we realize that we have already been crucified, we will apply the cross to ourselves; and when we realize by experience that the self has been buried, we as a person will be transferred into the spirit. Then we will not only exercise our spirit to contact the Lord, but our whole being will be in the spirit. So there are three strategic points that we need to pass: the altar, the first veil, and the second veil. At the altar our sins are dealt with; at the first veil the world is dealt with; and at the second veil we ourselves—the soulish life, the natural man, the outer man, the flesh, the self—are dealt with. Then we become a person in the spirit. This is beyond the mere exercise of our spirit to experience something of the Lord.

THE EXPERIENCE OF THE RED SEA
AND THE JORDAN RIVER

Let us look further into the geography and history of the children of Israel. In Egypt, the people of Israel partook of the Passover, which dealt with their sins. They were saved when their sins were dealt with by the Passover Lamb, but the Egyptian force, Pharaoh and his army, still enslaved them. So they had to pass through the Red Sea. Under the waters of the Red Sea, the worldly forces were buried. The army of Pharaoh includes a host of people and all the worldly things. With some people, a pair of eyeglasses is a soldier of the Egyptian army, because for them it is a worldly item. With others, the matter of dress is not only a single soldier, but a division of soldiers in the Egyptian army! Many worldly items bind and control us under their tyranny. But when Israel passed the Red Sea, the whole world was dealt with. All of the Egyptian army was buried under the water of the Red Sea. The water of the Red Sea typifies the first aspect of the effectiveness of Christ's death. All the worldly things are dealt with and buried in the death of Christ.

Later, after Israel left Egypt, they began wandering in the wilderness and daily enjoyed the manna, which was something heavenly of Christ. They could always testify to others how they enjoyed Christ, but at the same time they were wandering in the wilderness. One day, they passed through the Jordan River, and in the water of the Jordan twelve stones representing the old Israel were buried. Under the water of the Red Sea the Egyptian forces were buried, but under the water of the Jordan the self and the old man of the Israelites were buried. After this, they entered the third place, the land of Canaan, and enjoyed its all-inclusive riches.

When the people of Israel were in Egypt, they were in the outer court. When they came into the wilderness, they were in the holy place. Finally, when they entered into Canaan, they were in the Holiest of all. The Red Sea corresponds to the first veil, and the Jordan River to the second veil. It is very clear that these two waters typify the two aspects of the cross of Christ. The first aspect of the cross deals with all our worldly things, and the second aspect deals with the self in our soul. In other words, it is the cross that rends the two veils. We must pass through the two veils just as the Israelites had to pass through the two waters.

Now we must check ourselves and determine where we are. Are we in Egypt? in the wilderness? or in Canaan? In other words, are we in the outer court? in the holy place? or in the Holiest of all? Are we in the worldly atmosphere with everything under the sun? Those who are in the outer court do not have the light of the holy place—they only have the sun. All worldly things are under the sun. Are we such Christians who believe in the Lord Jesus, accept Him as Savior and believe that He died on the cross for our sins, and yet still have the worldly point of view and live in the worldly atmosphere? Or, are we in the holy place enjoying Christ day by day as our manna, our heavenly light, and our sweet savor of resurrection?

Or, are we deeper than this? In the Holiest of all we can experience Christ as the hidden one—not as Aaron in the outer court, but as Melchisedec in the heavenly Holiest of all. Here we may enjoy Christ as the hidden manna, as the hidden law, and as the hidden authority of resurrection in order to rule over all things. Everything here is hidden, because Christ is now experienced most deeply within. May the Lord be gracious to us that we may know where we are and where we need to go.

CHAPTER NINETEEN

THE HIDDEN CHRIST IN OUR SPIRIT

The tabernacle or the temple, as we have seen, is of three parts: the outer court, the holy place, and the Holiest of all. Within the outer court the tabernacle is divided into two parts: the holy place and the Holiest of all. Before we see the items in the Holiest of all, we must first look at those in the outer court and in the holy place.

THE OUTER COURT

In the outer court there are two things: the altar and the laver. All Bible students agree that the altar is the type of the cross of Christ and the laver is the type of the work of the Holy Spirit. Have we experienced the altar and the laver? On the cross Christ was offered as our sin offering. He died for our sins, and He was even made Sin on the cross for our sake; so He is our Passover. The meaning of the Passover is that He, the very Lamb of God, bore our sins and died on the cross. First Corinthians 5:7 clearly states that Christ is our Passover. The day that we believed in His death for our sins was the day of our Passover. It was on that day we enjoyed Christ as our Passover Lamb.

After we experienced the altar of the cross, immediately the Holy Spirit began to work, as signified by the laver. The laver is a place for people to be washed and cleansed. After receiving Christ as our Passover, the Holy Spirit starts His cleansing work within and without. When the people of Israel entered the tabernacle, they had to pass the altar with the sin and trespass offerings; but they also had to wash their feet and their hands of all the earthly dirt in the laver. The Holy Spirit cleanses us from all the earthly dirt of our daily walk since we were saved. If we have had these experiences, it means that we have been saved and are no longer outside the outer court. Once we are inside the outer court, we are within the boundary and realm of God. In other words, we are in the kingdom of God, for we have been regenerated, redeemed, forgiven, and now cleansed by the working of the Holy Spirit. Unless we have experienced both the altar and the laver, we can never be a real child of God. Even though we may have outwardly entered Christianity, without the experience of these two things we are still outside the kingdom of God.

THE HOLY PLACE

But this is not all; this is just the ABCs of the Christian life. We must press in further. We have entered the main gate of the tabernacle, but there is still another veil or gate which we must enter. From the outer court, from the place to which we came by believing in the Lord, we need to enter into the holy place.

The first item in the holy place is the *showbread table,* a table by which the bread is shown. The bread is a type of Christ as our food, for He is the Bread of Life (John 6:35). Christ is the supply for our life. He is our daily manna, nourishing us that we may live before God. The showbread table does not merely contain one piece of bread; it is a table holding a large amount of bread. This means we may experience an abundant supply of life, just as the manna which fell from heaven. Every morning there was an abundant supply of manna. Since we experienced Christ as our Passover and the cleansing work of the Holy Spirit, have we gone on to experience Christ as our daily manna? If we have, we know the showbread table in a living way.

The candlestick, or the *lampstand,* follows the showbread table as the second item. This means that Christ is the light as well as the life. John 1:4 says that life is in Christ, and this life is the very light of men. John 8:12 also states that this light is the light of life. If we can enjoy and experience Christ as life, then He will definitely become our light. When we feed on Christ, we can sense the shining within enlightening us. After we have received Christ as our Passover and have been cleansed by the working of the Holy Spirit, and after we know how to feed upon Christ as our daily manna of life, then we can sense the inner shining.

The third item, *the altar of incense,* follows the showbread table and the lampstand. This is experienced when we sense a savor, a sweetsmelling odor. This sweet odor, which is Christ in resurrection, spreads and ascends toward God. When we enjoy Christ as our food and are in His light of life, we are then in the resurrection. Within us there is something sweet spreading and ascending toward God. This can never be confirmed by knowledge or by doctrine, but must be checked by our experience. Do we have such experiences? Although we may not have enough of these experiences, the main issue at this time is that we have had such experiences. I can testify that it is wonderful! Thirty-three years ago I was daily and even hourly in this holy place. Oh, Christ was my daily manna and I was full of Him and full of light. I was very pleased with God and He was very pleased with me, and something of Christ within me was spreading and ascending to God as a sweet savor.

THE ARK IN THE HOLIEST OF ALL

But is this the end? This is something holy, but it is not the holiest. It is good, but it is not the best. Therefore, we need to press on again in order to enter into the Holiest of all. The first veil has to be passed through, but the second veil has to be rent. This veil is the flesh (Heb. 10:20), which must be broken before we can enter the Holiest of all.

There is only one thing in the Holiest place—that is *the ark.* All students of the Bible agree that the ark is a type of Christ. Although Christ may be enjoyed as our food, as our light, and as our sweet savor toward God, yet Christ *Himself* is in the Holiest of all. Christ as food, as light, and as the sweet savor are the three items in the holy place, but now Christ *Himself* has to be touched. We must not just touch Christ as some item, but Christ *Himself.* This is deeper. We must make contact with Christ Himself. We have experienced Christ as our Passover and the washing of the Holy Spirit; then we have experienced Christ as life, as light, and as the sweet savor; now we have to contact Christ Himself. Very few

Christians have ever entered into the Holiest of all in order to touch the ark, which is Christ Himself.

Now let us consider the contents of the ark. It is quite meaningful to see that *manna* is in the ark. It is not the open manna, but the hidden manna; not the manna displayed, but manna in the secret place. The hidden manna, no doubt, corresponds with the showbread. The difference, however, is this: the showbread is shown forth, but the manna in the ark is hidden. The showbread is exhibited on the table, but the manna in the ark is hidden in the golden pot. Not only is the manna hidden in the golden pot, but this pot is hidden in the ark. It is doubly hidden! In the wilderness the people of Israel enjoyed the manna, but the manna they enjoyed was public manna; it was manna fallen to the earth, not the manna hidden in the heavens. The hidden manna is Christ Himself.

We need to experience such a deeper Christ, a Christ in the secret place, a Christ in the heavenlies. This is the Christ mentioned in Hebrews 7, according to the order of Melchisedec—not according to the order of Aaron. Aaron is in the outer court offering sacrifices upon the altar; Melchisedec is on the throne of grace in the heavenlies. We may experience Christ as our food, but this enjoyment is only in the holy place, and whatever we experience is immediately known by many people. Sometimes the news of our "glorious" experience spreads across the whole nation. This is nothing but the experience of the open showbread. We need to press deeper into the secret place of the Almighty in order to touch the heavenly Christ Himself.

In the ark is also the *law,* the regulating and enlightening law. The law corresponds with the lampstand in the holy place. The law is the testimony of God, and the lampstand in both the Old Testament and the New Testament is also the testimony of God. Though the law corresponds with the lampstand, the principle is still the same: the lampstand shines forth openly, but this law is a hidden, inner, and deeper light. Many times the brothers and sisters have only the light of the lampstand. Oh, how their light shines! In one sense that is good, but in another sense they are still shallow; everything is showing forth on the surface. They need Christ to become their inner law. Those who have Christ as their living law hidden within them do not show forth much outwardly, but inwardly know Christ in a deeper way.

Thirdly, the *budded rod* is in the ark. The rod, with sprouted buds, typifies the resurrected Christ. This corresponds with the savor of the incense, both of which signify the resurrected Christ; but again the difference is that the incense is openly expressed, whereas the budded rod is experienced in a hidden and deeper way.

Three things have been seen in the holy place: Christ as food, Christ as life, and Christ as the sweet savor. But the three things in the ark of the Holiest place are deeper. The showbread is something *showing forth,* the lampstand is something *shining forth,* and the incense is something *spreading forth*—all are outwardly exhibited. But the three things in the ark are deeply and inwardly hidden.

PRESSING DEEPER INTO CHRIST

We are now clear that the holy place represents the wilderness on one hand and the soul on the other. In ancient times the Israelites were originally in Egypt. Since it was in Egypt that they experienced the Passover, Egypt was their outer court. After the Passover, they were brought out of Egypt into the wilderness. In other words, they proceeded from the outer court into the holy place.

While the holy place corresponds to the wilderness for the Israelites, it corresponds to the human soul for the Corinthian and Hebrew believers. For example, the believers in Corinth had experienced Christ as their Passover (1 Cor. 5:7), and then passed into the wilderness in their experience, where they enjoyed Christ as their manna and as their living water (1 Cor. 10:1-5). They too were in the wilderness, just as the Israelites of old, but the wilderness for the Corinthians was the soul. By reading 1 Corinthians carefully, we see that they were soulish and carnal. Yes, they enjoyed Christ as their food and as their light and had many wonderful experiences of Christ, but their enjoyment of Christ was in their souls. Their flesh, the veil that separates the Holiest of all from the holy place, had not been broken. Their souls had not

been dealt with, so they were not in the spirit, which is the
Holiest of all. They enjoyed something of Christ, but not
Christ Himself.

The Hebrew Christians also were typified by the Israelites
in the wilderness (Heb. 3:6-8). The Apostle Paul pointed out
to the Hebrew Christians as well as to the Corinthians that
the people of Israel were the illustration of their own condition. Chapter four of Hebrews indicates that to enter into the
rest is to enter into the Holiest of all and touch the throne of
grace, where Christ our High Priest is today. The Hebrew
Christians enjoyed something of Christ by the teachings.
First Corinthians deals with the matter of gifts, whereas
Hebrews deals with the matter of doctrines. The Corinthian
believers were *in the soul* enjoying the gifts, and the Hebrew
Christians were also *in the soul* enjoying the doctrines; therefore, they could not understand the deeper things. Since both
the Corinthians and Hebrews were addicted either to their
gifts or to the elementary doctrines, they had to tolerate the
wilderness in their souls.

This is why the Apostle Paul entreated the Corinthian
believers to know the spirit and be a spiritual man instead of
a soulish man (1 Cor. 2:11-15). And, in Hebrews 4:12, he said
the same thing—that they must divide or discern the spirit
from the soul. The principle in these two books is the same.
Only these two books in the New Testament refer to the history of Israel in the wilderness. The reason for this is that the
Corinthians were soulish in their gifts and the Hebrews were
soulish in their doctrines. Many Christians today are soulish
in their gifts and many others are soulish in their doctrines.
Without a doubt, the doctrines helped the Hebrew Christians
and the gifts helped the Corinthians. But they were all in the
soul, which is the holy place—not in the spirit, the Holiest of
all, where they could touch and experience Christ Himself. If
we are going to make contact with Him in our spirit, we have
to forsake our soul. We should not remain in the soul. If we
remain in the soul, we are wandering in the wilderness.

You may say, "Well, why is it important? I still enjoy something of Christ. Why do you say these doctrines are only
elementary? By them I know something about Christ and

enjoy something of Him. You say these gifts are stressed too much. Why, then, do I still enjoy something of Christ by the gifts?" Look at the picture in the wilderness. For more than thirty-eight years, the Israelites wandered in the wilderness, and day by day, through all that time, they partook of the manna. God is so merciful! He is not a small God, but an exceedingly generous God. Even when they were wrong, He still granted them something. But the manna, falling from the heavens daily, did not justify the wandering of the people of Israel in the wilderness. On the contrary, it proved how babyish and carnal they were by enjoying nothing more than manna for thirty-eight years. Manna was all right for a short time; but they should have soon left it to enjoy the produce of Canaan.

The lesson for us is simply this: to have the gifts for a short time is permissible, but to insist on having the gifts all the time only proves that we are babyish. We must go on and even press on. The gifts are not our portion—Christ is the portion that God has allotted us. Before the Apostle Paul dealt with the gifts in 1 Corinthians, he pointed out that Christ Himself is our portion. We are not called into the fellowship of *gifts,* but we are called into the fellowship of *Christ* (1 Cor. 1:9). God did not make the gifts our wisdom, but He made Christ our wisdom. It is through Christ that we are justified and sanctified and redeemed (1 Cor. 1:30). We have to thank God for His gifts, but they are only a help for a short time. Israel surely could thank God for their daily manna; but the manna was only a temporary provision until they arrived in the land. They should not have remained in the wilderness with the manna every day for thirty-eight years. Praise God for His wisdom and mercy, and thank God for His gifts, for when we are wandering in the wilderness, we do need the daily manna and gifts to help us. But this does not justify our continuing in such a course over an extended period of time. On the contrary, it may prove that we are still young and even babyish. If we would press on, there would be no further need for us to enjoy the manna; we could begin immediately to enjoy the produce of the good land of Canaan. When we enjoy the produce of the good land, it proves that we are in the rest and in the spirit. Otherwise, we are like Israel, remaining in the wilderness of our soul. If we are not in the spirit, the cross must deal with our flesh and our soul.

Hebrews 4, 5, and 6 exhort us to press on, and 1 Corinthians 9 exhorts us to run the race. We must press on to enter the spirit in order to touch Christ Himself and experience the deeper Christ as the hidden manna, the inner law, and the secret budding rod. The writer of 1 Corinthians advised the Corinthian believers to adjust and limit themselves with the gifts. They must learn how to use the gifts in a proper way (1 Cor. 14). If we read 1 Corinthians carefully and objectively, we will see that the intention of the writer is not to encourage, but to adjust the believers in the practice of gifts. In order to run the race in a proper way, we must know the deeper things of Christ in the spirit.

Now we all have to check where we are. Are we at the altar or the laver? Perhaps we are even outside the main gate! Have we experienced these two items in the outer court and gone on to the showbread table, the light and the sweet savor? Or, have we passed through the holy place and now are in the Holiest of all? If so, we are in the spirit, touching and experiencing Christ Himself in the deepest way. May the Lord be merciful to us so that we may know where we are.

CHAPTER TWENTY

TRIPARTITE MAN AND THE CHURCH

We must remember that God's economy and the mark of His economy is to dispense Himself into us. We were made in three parts: the body outwardly, the spirit inwardly, and the soul between. God's intention is to dispense Himself into the spirit of man, and then work Himself into man's soul.

TRIPARTITE MAN COMPLICATED BY THREE PERSONS

Before God could fulfill His intention, Satan, the enemy of God, wrought himself into the body of man. Thus, in the members of the body there is Sin—Sin personified. As an illegal king, it can overrule and force us to do things against our will. Satan himself, as the evil nature and as the law of sin, dwells in us to corrupt our body. The flesh is the body poisoned by Satan, and in us, that is in our flesh, *dwells* no good thing (Rom. 7:18). Our flesh serves the law of sin against our mind and against our will (Rom. 7:15, 20).

Satan came into our body as the law of sin; but, praise the Lord, when we were saved, the Triune God came to dwell in our spirit as our life. Christ as our *life* is in our spirit. What then is in our soul? *Self.* Our *self* is in our soul. Have we been impressed that all three beings—Adam, Satan, and God—are in us today? We are quite complicated. The man, Adam, is in us; the devil, Satan, is in us; and the Lord of life, God Himself, is in us. Hence, we have become a little garden of Eden. Adam representing the human race, the tree of life representing God, and the tree of knowledge representing Satan are the three parties in the garden of Eden; and now they are all in us. Adam, the self, is in our *soul;* Satan, the devil, is in our *body;* and God, the Triune God, is in our *spirit.* But we are more than a little garden; we are a great battlefield. Satan is in us fighting against God, and God is in us fighting against Satan. Satan takes our body, which is the flesh, as the base for his battles; God takes our spirit as the base for His warfare.

Galatians 5:17 says, "the flesh lusteth against the Spirit." In the Greek interlinear text "spirit" is written with a small letter. This means our flesh lusteth against our spirit and our spirit against the flesh. These two are contrary to one another, so we cannot do the things we desire. The corrupted flesh fights against the spirit, and the spirit fights against the flesh. These two parties are always warring with one another. Satan is in our flesh as Sin and the Triune God is in our spirit as Life, and day by day there is a spiritual warfare raging between them in the battlefield of our soul.

TRIPARTITE MAN REPRESENTED BY THE MIND

As we have seen, there are three parts in the soul: the mind, the emotion, and the will. The mind as the thinking organ of the soul represents the self. What we think and consider always precedes what we do; therefore, our mind represents our "self." This is why Romans 7, 8, and 12 deal with the mind. Romans 7 tells us that the mind stands with the law of God. My mind desires to keep the law of God and by itself desires to serve God (Rom. 7:25); but my mind, representing myself, is too weak. I myself am too weak. Whenever I make up my mind to do good, there is something else stronger than myself, stronger than my mind—that is, the sinful one in the flesh. Whenever I exercise my mind to do the will of God and keep the law of God, the evil one in my members rises up against me, defeats me and brings me into captivity (Rom. 7:23). My mind, representing myself, cannot keep the law of God; if my mind tries to do the will of God by itself, it is always defeated.

The mind in Romans 7 is an independent mind, trying to do good by itself; so the Apostle brings us into chapter 8 and tells us how the mind must be dependent. The independent mind, trying to do things under its own power, will be defeated. On what then must the mind be dependent?

Romans 8:6 says, "To set the mind on the flesh is death, but to set the mind on the spirit is life and peace" (R.S.V.). There are two possibilities for the mind: it may depend either on the flesh or on the spirit. If it depends on the flesh, the result will be death; but if it depends on the spirit, there will be life and peace. Have we seen the difference between the independent mind in chapter 7 and the dependent mind in chapter 8? An independent mind will be defeated, but a mind dependent on the spirit will have victory. Since there are two parties within us—Satan in our members and the Triune God in our spirit—we can no longer be really independent; so we should never try. If we do, we will surely be defeated. If we attempt to defeat the enemy, we will eventually be defeated by him. We must therefore turn in dependence to another One, to the Triune God within our spirit. The key to victory is to always set our mind upon the spirit.

We must all be impressed with this clear picture: Satan is in us, Christ is in us, and self stands in the middle. The enemy tempts us to do good by our own efforts, and the usual response is: "I love the Lord and belong to the Lord, so I want to do good to please Him." This is the temptation! When we are independent and making up our minds to do good by our own strength, we are being tempted, and we will surely be defeated. We may be able to do good today, tomorrow, and possibly even for three days, but we certainly cannot keep it up for three and a half days. The lesson we need to learn is never to be independent and try to do things in our strength, but always depend upon the Lord. Whenever we are tempted to do good by our own effort, we had better tell the enemy: "No, Satan, No! I cannot and will not go that way. I don't know anything about doing good; I only know one thing—to depend upon my Lord. I will not be drawn away from leaning upon Him." Then we will have the victory and life and peace. It is really simple. The Triune God has dispensed Himself into our spirit as our life and as everything to us; therefore, we must learn never to do anything independently or anything in our own strength.

Before we leave these two chapters of Romans we must see something about the laws. We have seen that Sin is in the flesh, and with Sin there is also a law, the evil law of sin. We all know what a law is. If I pick up a book and throw it into the air, it will inevitably fall to the earth. This is the law of gravity. But let me do something against this law, such as to lift a book with my hand and hold it in this position for two or three hours. I can sustain it for a while, but finally I will have to give up. Why? Because my own effort cannot stand against the law of gravity. Our personal effort cannot contradict the natural law. In the morning we may say to ourselves, "I have to be patient. I must not lose my temper. I have to endure for a whole day." Perhaps we can be patient for even two days, but on the third day we will lose a "big" temper. To lose our temper is the law of sin; not to lose the temper is our own effort. To be proud is also a law operating within us. None of us has ever graduated from the school of pride. Even a little child knows how to be proud. The parents have never taught their children to be proud—how can they be proud? It comes by "nature," and that sinful "nature" is the law, the law of sin within us.

Let us go back to the illustration of holding the book in the air. It would be foolish to exert my effort to hold that book in the air when I see a table in front of me. The table represents another law—the law of a solid support versus the law of gravity. I can lay the book on the table and shout "Hallelujah!" I can leave it there and be in peace. The book is perfectly safe on the table, because the law of a solid support overcomes the law of gravity. Who is the real support? It is Christ, the *Rock*. Where is He? He is in our *spirit*. Therefore, we can set our mind upon the spirit, and leave the "book" upon the Table. Forget about your effort. Never make up your mind to do good. Never say, "Oh, before, I was so cruel to my husband (or wife, or someone else); now, today, I determine to be kind." We may be kind for a day or two, but we cannot last much longer than that. Never try to make any resolutions. It does not work. Within us is Christ, the everlasting Rock. He is in us as the "table," as our Rock. We should just set our minds upon Him all the time, leave ourselves upon the Rock, and go to sleep. This is the way of victory and release. When we set our mind upon the spirit, we simply hand ourselves over to

Christ. When we rely upon Him, we simply say to Him, "Lord, here I am, hopeless and helpless. From now on I will never try to make up my mind to do anything. I give my mind to You. I set my mind upon You." By doing this, we are handing ourselves over to the Lord. The Lord will then have the ground and the opportunity to spread Himself through us and saturate us with Himself. How wonderful!

TRIPARTITE MAN REALIZES THE BODY LIFE

Now we go on from Romans 8 to Romans 12. Chapters 9, 10, and 11 are parenthetical chapters; so chapter 12 is the continuation of chapter 8. In chapter 7 the mind was independent, but in chapter 8 the mind is dependent—dependent on the spirit. The mind in chapter 7 represents the independent self struggling by its own effort, which always ends in defeat. The mind in chapter 8 represents the dependent self resting upon the Lord Jesus. This gives the Lord opportunity to saturate our whole being with Himself, causing us to become a *living* member of His Body. We are then brought to chapter 12. Chapter 12 deals with three things for the realization of the proper church life: the body, the mind, which is the main part of the soul, and the spirit.

(1) Our Body Presented for the Church Life

Once we rely upon Christ and He takes possession of our whole being, our body is *released* from the usurping hand of the enemy. When we lived independently, Satan could take possession of our body and force us to do things against our will. Now, as we rely upon Christ, the strongest One, He releases our body from the enemy's usurping hand. Then what is the next step? We must present our body to the Lord (Rom. 12:1). This is one thing many dear Christian brothers and sisters have not yet done. We must *present* our body definitely to Him, saying: "Lord, I thank You that my body, which was formerly a body of sin and a body under death, is now quickened and released. I present this body to You for Your Body. If I keep my body in my hands, Your Body cannot be realized." If we are going to realize the Body of Christ, we must definitely and practically present our body to Christ.

In these days, while travelling from coast to coast, I have met a good number of Christians who are talking about the Body life. But how about *our* body? We talk so much about the Body of Christ, but what are we doing with our body? Are we still keeping it in our own hands? As long as our body is kept in our hands, there is no possibility for us to realize the Body of Christ. In Romans 12 we are told that if we desire to realize the church life, we must first present our released body to the Lord. Since it is no longer our body, it must be presented to the Lord as a living sacrifice.

Brothers, do we come to the meetings with our *heart* or with our *body?* So many Christians say, "Oh, I do have a heart for the church life!" Yes, they may have a heart for the church life, but their body is not for the church life. Their body is left at home. We must be able to say, "I not only have a heart for the church life, but I also have a body for the church life." Is our heart for the church life and our body for our private life? If so, how can we realize the church life? We can talk very nicely about it: everything is "Hallelujah" and everyone is in the "heavenlies"! But actually everything is just in the "air" and in the heart. If we are going to realize the Body life of Christ, we must definitely present our body to the Lord. "Lord, formerly my body was under the usurping hand of the enemy. Now I thank You, You have released this body. Here, I present it to You. It is no longer my body, but Your sacrifice!" Then we will be able to realize the church life.

(2) Our Mind Renewed for the Church Life

After we present our body to the Lord, the second thing for the realization of the church life must promptly take place. We must be transformed by the renewing of our mind (Rom. 12:2). Formerly, our mind always tried to do something by itself for God; now it relies upon Christ. This mind which depends on the Lord must be renewed, enlightened, and re-educated.

Here is a real example. A brother, who really loves the Lord and the church life, definitely offered his body as a sacrifice to the Lord and to the church. But, after he presented himself, he became a big problem to the church. When he was indifferent about the church life, the church was at peace; but now, when his body comes to the church, his mind comes also, and his mind has not yet been renewed. The old things of Christianity have not yet been crossed out and purged. When he did not present his body, he was indifferent about the church. He said, "If I have time and I feel like it, I will come to the meetings. If I don't, I just won't come." But now he loves the Lord more, so he has presented himself to the Lord and the church. He has put himself wholly into the church. But as his body comes, so does his troublesome mind, bringing with it many opinions, teachings, thoughts, and various considerations, which cause much trouble to the church life.

After the *body* is presented, the *mind* must be renewed. When we take our full share in the practical life of the church, we must have our mind purged, renewed, and re-educated. To have our mind renewed and re-educated, we must drop all our old thoughts and natural ideas and all the teachings and considerations of traditional Christianity. This is what it means to be transformed by the renewing of the mind. Then the church life is possible; otherwise, the mind will be the biggest problem and the greatest source of trouble in the church. Some dear ones have brought in so many problems since they came into the church. Before they came, the church was very much at peace and in unity, but since they came in, their minds have created trouble for the church. They think, "My heart is good"; but actually their minds are terrible. Many old things have to be stripped off for the transforming of their minds.

(3) Our Spirit Fervent for the Church Life

First of all, the body must be presented; then the mind, representing the soul, needs to be renewed; and finally, the spirit must be on fire, burning fervently. We have to be fervent in the spirit (Rom. 12:11). A dear brother may have presented his body to the Lord and to the church and may be entirely renewed in his mind, for all the old things have been dropped; but he may be so cold in the spirit! He is no more a problem, but he becomes a burden. Every time he comes to the meeting, he sits there as cold as the grave. He is always quiet and never troublesome, but the church must bear him as a burden.

When responsibility is shared in the elders' or deacons' meeting, he just sits there. His attitude is: "I am totally with you and I am for the church. I have no problem; whatever you brothers say is all right with me." Suppose when the responsible brothers meet together they are all like this. Who will bear the burden? All those brothers become themselves a burden, not one bearing their share of the church's burden. On one hand we should not be troublesome, but on the other hand we need to be a troublemaker. In other words, we should have no variance, no crosscurrent with the brothers, but we should be on fire. We should be burned and burning. *We must be fervent in our spirit.*

The Christian life may seem to be individual and private, but really it is not; it is a corporate life, a body life. You alone are not the Body; you are a member, and you need others as members in order to realize the church life. When we stop trying to do good by ourselves and learn to depend on Christ and live by Him, we are a living member and prepared to be a functioning member of His Body. Then we have to realize the church life by definitely presenting our body to the Lord, by having our mind renewed, and by having our spirit on fire. When the body is presented, the soul transformed, and the spirit on fire, then we will have the church life. We will be a living, functioning member—not a troublesome, cold, or dead member. We will not be a member *out of* function, but a prevailing and aggressive member *in* function. We will have the reality of the church life.

Chapter Twenty-One

THE BUILDING OF GOD'S DWELLING PLACE

There are many more important details to consider about the spirit and the soul, but now our attention must be focused on the building of God's dwelling place. Much stress has been made on the tabernacle, God's dwelling place. We have seen that it is composed of the outer court and the two parts of the tent of the tabernacle, the holy place and the Holiest of all. Let us briefly review the contents of these three places.

In the outer court there is the altar, which typifies the cross of Christ, and the laver, which typifies the cleansing work of the Holy Spirit.

The holy place contains the showbread table, the lampstand, and the incense altar. These three items are types of the various aspects of Christ as our life. The showbread table reveals Christ as our daily life supply—He is our very bread of life. The candlestick, or the lampstand, typifies Christ as the light of life. The supply of life that we enjoy becomes the light, which shines within us. Next, the incense altar typifies the resurrection savor of Christ.

The Holiest of all contains one thing, the ark, the type of Christ Himself. There are three things within the ark: the hidden manna, which is the inner life and inner life supply; the hidden law, which is the inner enlightening within us; and the hidden rod with sprouted buds, which is the inner resurrection power and authority. The hidden manna, the hidden law, and the hidden authority are all in resurrection and are much deeper than the three corresponding items in the holy place.

THE CONTENTS OF THE TABERNACLE

All these things are the contents of the tabernacle, the dwelling place of God. The experiences of all these eight items in the outer court, the holy place, and the Holiest of all are the real contents of the true building of God, the Church. If we desire to be the building of God's dwelling place, we must experience what Christ has accomplished by His cross and the cleansing of the Holy Spirit. We must also adequately experience Christ as our life, our light, and our resurrection savor. Furthermore, we must have real experiences of Christ *Himself* as the hidden manna, the hidden law, and the hidden authority. The experience of Christ in all these aspects forms the real content of the building of God and provides the very materials for the building.

In these last few years people have been talking so much about the New Testament Church. But the New Testament Church is not a Church of a certain pattern, but one of life and of experiences of Christ. Suppose we should say, "Let us pattern a man after that person." So we make an arm out of wax, a head out of marble, a torso with wood, and the legs and feet with some clay. Once these are put together in the exact size and shape and painted in the exact color, we may have the true *pattern* of that man, but we do not have the reality of that man. The real man is not *manufactured* according to pattern, but *born* and *matured* by the growth of life. This man was first born of a living mother and then grew by receiving daily nourishment. Ultimately he became such a man with a certain pattern. If otherwise, there may be the pattern, but not the man.

One time when we were in Pittsburgh, I said to a friend, "Let us forget about the pattern and pay full attention to the life. For example, you have a nice little boy. You don't pay much attention to his pattern. You don't try to shape him day by day in a particular way. First, he is born of his mother, and then you nourish him with milk and baby food. The baby then grows and grows, assuming a certain shape and pattern. That pattern comes out of his birth and growth of life. Just as we could not form your child, so neither can we form a New Testament Church. If we try to form it, all we have is a pattern without the life. It is possible for us to form a church of pattern, but we cannot form a church of life."

During the last few years I have been continually urging people and pleading with people: *"Don't form anything!"* Whatever we form is not the real Church. Not one living person on this earth through the past six thousand years has been formed; every one had a birth and the growth of life. The Church is the Body of Christ, and no human hand can form it. We can form many things, but we cannot form a living Body composed of living members. We are never commanded or instructed in the New Testament to form the Church; but we are exhorted to experience Christ, to minister Christ to others, and to bring forth many children by spiritual birth. The real Church, the Body of Christ, only comes out of birth and the growth of life. This is why we stress the principle that the *tabernacle comes out of the experiences of the contents*.

THE SEPARATION OF THE OUTER COURT

Based on this principle, let us see what are the main materials of the tabernacle. First of all, there is "the separation" of the outer court (Exo. 27:9-19; 38:9-20). It is called "the separation" because it is like the fence surrounding your property, separating and keeping it from all that is outside. The separation of the outer court is made of three main things: 1) the brass sockets, 2) the pillars, and 3) the hangings made of fine, twined linen. The base of the separating walls is made of the sockets of brass. There are twenty sockets on the north side, another twenty on the south side, ten on the west side at the rear, and ten at the front (Exo. 27)—altogether sixty sockets of brass. On each of these sockets stands a pillar, all of which are connected and united with links. The hangings on the pillars are made of fine linen, twined together with two threads. Therefore, the three main things are the brass sockets, the pillars, and the fine, twined linen hangings.

The brass which forms the base of the separation is the same material as that of the two things seen in the outer court: the brass altar and the brass laver. The spiritual meaning is that the brass sockets come from the experience of the altar and the laver. Both the altar and the laver are made out of brass; therefore, all the sockets of separation are made of brass. Within the outer court are the brass altar, the brass laver, and the brass sockets. The immediate impression people receive when they come into the outer court is that the base of the separation is brass, the same material of which the altar and the laver are made. This means that the experiences of the cross and the cleansing of the Holy Spirit are the very base for the separation of the Lord's building.

We know that brass in type is God's divine judgment. All that we have, all that we are, and all that we do must be put on the altar to be judged. The altar, or the cross, is first a place of judgment; God judged everything on the cross. The brass used to overlay this altar, according to Numbers 16, came from the brass censers of the 250 rebellious people. When these people who rebelled against God and Moses were judged with fire, God told Moses to pick up all their brass censers to make a cover for the altar as a memorial. This was a memorial of God's judgment on the rebellious (Num. 16:38). In order to realize the building of the Church, all that we have, all that we can do, and all that we are need to be judged by the cross of Christ. This is the separating base of sockets for God's building.

Perhaps we are clear about the principle of separation, but we are not able to apply it. Suppose I am a brother who was saved in today's Christianity. Through the preaching of the Gospel I heard that I was a sinner, that Christ loved me, and that He died on the cross. As a result, I admitted that I was a sinner. I prayed, "Oh God, forgive me for I am sinful. I thank Thee that Thou hast given Thy Son, the Lord Jesus, to die on the cross for me. I praise Thee that He is my Savior and that my sins are forgiven. Hallelujah! I have joy and peace within me." Of course, I then went to a pastor, who was a good friend of mine, and allowed him to baptize me. After being baptized, I became a "member" of his church. One day the Lord opened my eyes to see why He saved me. He saved me for the purpose of being built up together with others to become the dwelling place of God. After hearing a group of believers in my locality talk about the Body life and the building up of the church, I was willing to built up with them in the Body life. Finally, the Holy Spirit said to me, "Do you come to be built up? Do you come to realize the church life? Then you must first go to the

cross! All that you can do, all that you are, and all that you
have must be judged on the cross." I then must confess and
repent saying, "Lord, *nothing* of me is acceptable to Thee, and
nothing is good for Thy building. All has to be judged." If I do
not follow through with the judgment of the cross, it is impossible for me to be built up with others; there is no base, no
foundation. If I come into the church proudly, it is possible for
me to be organized, but it is impossible for me to be built up in
the church. The foundation, as seen in the sockets of the separation of God's building, comes from the experience of the
brass altar. Thus, the solid foundation of the building of God's
dwelling place comes from the experience of the cross. There is
no other way. All must be put on the altar and burned and
judged. At the main entrance of the church is the cross. If we
are going to enter into the church, we must put ourselves on
the altar of the cross.

When our whole being and all our actions have been put
on the cross, we can testify how dirty, how worldly, and how
sinful we are. We realize that we not only need Christ's
redemption, but also the cleansing of the Holy Spirit. One day
according to my inner sense I felt like jumping into the laver.
I prayed: "Lord, cleanse me! I am sinful, I am worldly! Every
bit of me is dirty! I need the cleansing of the Holy Spirit!" By
this burden in prayer, I experienced the cross and the laver.
At the cross we put everything of ourselves to death, and at
the laver we put everything under the cleansing power of the
Holy Spirit. This not only makes us pure, but purged. Then
we will come humbly to the church by His mercy, by His
redemption, and by His cleansing. After a brother experiences the altar and the laver, and after he is purified from all
pride and self-righteousness, he has the base, the sockets of
brass, upon which the pillar is erected.

The Scripture does not tell us of what material the pillars
were made, but we are told that the hooks and the fillets that
fasten the pillars together and the capitals that overlay the
pillars were made of silver. Silver typifies redemption. This
signifies that for God's building we are all joined and united
together and covered by nothing other than the Lord's
redemption. If we are going to practice the church life, we

have to realize that it is by the Lord's redemption that we are united, and under this redemption we are covered that we may be separated for God's building.

Upon the pillars are also the hangings of fine, twined linen, giving people the testimony that the Church is so pure and clean in conduct and behavior. This is the separating line. If the tabernacle is erected with the surrounding separating line, one can see from afar the white linen demarcating it. That is the testimony of the Church to a world that is in darkness. The whole world is black, but here is something erected, testifying that the Church is clean, pure, and white. This kind of testimony can only come from the judgment of the altar and the cleansing of the laver, which results in a pure behavior and unsullied conduct before the world. This is the fine, twined linen hanging upon the supporting pillars which are based upon the sockets of brass. This is the separating line of testimony that the Church is purged from the world. Outside this line everything is black, but within this line everything is white.

THE BOARDS OF THE TABERNACLE

Although this is good, it is only the experience of the outer court. There are a number of good things in the outer court: brass, silver, and white linen. *But there is nothing of gold,* which is the type of the divine nature. This means that when we are in the outer court nothing of the divine nature has yet been wrought into us that could be expressed. There is only the judging and purging away of the negative things. In other words, a brother who was so proud when he came to us is now very humble and seems to have no self-righteousness, self-glory, and pride. But this is just something in the realm of human conduct and its purifying. There is nothing of God wrought into him that could be expressed—there is no gold manifested. It is good on the outside; but this is only the court, not the building. This is still in the open air, with no shelter, no covering, no building. We need something divine to be mingled with our nature: we need the mingling of divinity with humanity. Therefore, we must press on from the outer court to the holy place and even to the Holiest of all.

If by the mercy and grace of the Lord we enter into the holy place and the Holiest of all, nearly everywhere we will see gold—a golden table, a golden lampstand, a golden incense altar, the golden ark, and golden boards. All the surroundings are gold, the contents are gold, and every piece of the utensils is gold. What is the meaning of this? Praise the Lord, the wood of the boards (Exo. 26:15) signifies humanity, the human nature; and the gold overlaying the boards signifies divinity, the divine nature. Now divinity and humanity have become one! On one hand it is wood, and on the other hand it is gold. Here within the holy place and the Holiest of all, divinity is mingled with humanity. That is why they are called the holy place and the Holiest of all, for anything holy must be of God. In the outer court we are righteous, but not holy. Every aspect of our behavior and conduct in the outer court is right, for it is judged at the cross and purified at the laver. There is righteousness there, but not holiness, which is the divine nature wrought into man. Not until we enter into the holy place and the Holiest of all do we see everything overlaid with gold. Nearly everything, every part, has the element of wood, but is overlaid with gold. Humanity is there, but it is mingled with the divine nature.

Unless we enter into the holy place and the Holiest of all and have something divine wrought into us, it is impossible for us to be the boards built up together as the dwelling place of God. The Church is built with the mingling of God with man. *The mingling of God Himself with us becomes the very material* for the building of the Body of Christ. No matter how much we have been purified, we can only be the white linen; we cannot be the boards for the building of the tabernacle. But the more we are overlaid with gold, the more we become the materials for the building of God. This is why we must enter into the spirit, exercise our spirit, walk after the spirit, and always be mingled with the Lord in the spirit. It is by this mingling of divinity with humanity that we become the materials for the building of the house of God.

The boards overlaid with gold in the holy place and the Holiest of all are based upon silver sockets, which means that Christ's redemption is the basis and foundation for the building of God's house. But from where does the gold for the boards come? It comes from the experiences of the golden table, the golden lampstand, the golden incense altar, and the golden ark. The more we experience Christ as our life, as our light, and as our resurrection savor, and the more we experience Christ Himself in the deepest way, the more the divine nature is wrought into us. The gold which overlays the boards comes from the very experience of the contents of the holy place and the Holiest of all. The divinity that is mingled with our humanity only comes from the experience of Christ as our life, our light, and our resurrection savor, and even from the deepest experience of Christ Himself. This forms the materials for God's building. We must experience *Christ* daily as our manna, as our light, as our resurrection savor, and experience Himself in the deepest way in order to gain the divine mingling.

In order to be built up there are at least three other things about which we must be clear. Firstly, each board is one and a half cubits wide (Exo. 26:16). We must realize that we are just one and a half cubits and no more. There are forty-eight boards in the tabernacle, which are combined in pairs, each pair of boards measuring three cubits in width. The reason why each board is only one and a half cubits wide is that each is only half the full measure and needs to be matched by another board. We must realize that we are only a half. When the Lord Jesus sent His disciples, He always sent them out by twos. Peter needed John, and John needed Peter. We are only a half and need another half to complete us. We should never act and work independently or individually. All our service and function in the church must be accomplished in a corporate way. Two boards must be put together. We are not a complete whole; we need another half. Who is your other half? We must realize that each one of us is not three cubits, but simply one and a half cubits. We cannot go alone, we cannot serve individually, we cannot function and work independently. We must be a coordinated member in the building of God.

Furthermore, each board has two tenons, two extra parts stretching into the sockets (Exo. 26:19). Why are there two tenons instead of one for each board? It is clear. One tenon would allow the board to spin around, but two tenons hold it firmly in place. Two means confirmation. It is like a person with two feet. If a man stands on one foot it is easy for him to turn or fall, but with a stance of two feet it is not so easy to fall and it is awkward to turn around. We don't like to have so many "turning around" brothers. In the morning one may be facing one direction, and in the afternoon toward the opposite direction. By the next morning he has turned yet another way—always turning around. If we don't know where he is, we can never catch him. He is always spinning around on one tenon. With these unstable brothers and sisters there can be no building. They must become stable. No matter what happens, they must stand there until death. When a person is willing to sacrifice his life, then the building of the church is possible. Others are needed to match us, and we need their confirmation continually.

Besides this, there are the golden bars and the golden rings that connect and unite all the boards together as one. The rings represent the Holy Spirit. We received the Holy Spirit as the rings at the very beginning of our Christian life when we were regenerated (Luke 15:22 and Gen. 24:47). The rings hold the bars, which also typify the Holy Spirit, but with the human nature—within the golden bars is the acacia wood. As we have already seen, after the resurrection and ascension of the Lord, the Holy Spirit came down from heaven with both the divine nature and the human nature; thus He is now the Spirit of Jesus. It is this wonderful Holy Spirit with both the divine and human natures who combines and unites us together. All the boards then become as one. Suppose all the gold is removed from the boards, the rings, and the bars. Then, with all the gold stripped away, all the boards will become disconnected, individual pieces. The oneness is not in the wood but in the gold. If the gold is taken, there is no uniting element, and the boards are left as separate and individual pieces. By this picture we can clearly see that the unity, the oneness, the building up are not in the wood, but wholly in the gold. This means that the building up of the Church is not in the human nature, but in the divine nature. It is in the divine nature that we are all built together. It is the divine nature that joins us, unites us, and holds us together as one.

You and I must learn, first of all, that we are just a half; secondly, we must never act independently and individually without the confirmation of others. Finally, we must act, live, and serve in the divine nature. It is in the divine nature that we as the boards are united together as one. Then we will have the building of God. Again, it must be repeated that all of this comes from the experiences of Christ as the show-bread, as the lamp, as the resurrection savor, and as the very ark including the hidden manna, the hidden law, and the hidden rod. How meaningful this is! May the Lord fully, deeply, and wholly impress us with this picture. This is the right way for us to be built up together as the dwelling place of God. The Church is not a matter of a pattern, but the real experience of Christ as our life and everything; therefore, the only way for the Church to be built up among us is to experience Christ in the spirit.

Chapter Twenty-Two

THE COVERING OF GOD'S BUILDING

"Moreover thou shalt make the tabernacle with ten curtains; of fine twined linen, and blue, and purple, and scarlet, with cherubim the work of the skilful workman shalt thou make them."

"And thou shalt make curtains of goats' hair for a tent over the tabernacle: eleven curtains shalt thou make them....And thou shalt make a covering for the tent of rams' skins dyed red, and a covering of sealskins above" (Exo. 26:1, 7, 14).

From the above passages we learn that there are four layers forming the covering of the tabernacle. The first layer consists of ten curtains of fine linen; the second is composed of curtains of goats' hair; the third is a covering of rams' skins, and the fourth is the outside covering of badgers or seals' skins. These four layers of coverings form the roof of the tabernacle. Much has been written by others about the tabernacle and its coverings, but my burden is to point out how these coverings are related to the Lord's building.

THE CHURCH BUILT BY CHRIST AS LIFE

In the previous chapter we saw that the Lord's building is not merely a pattern, but a matter of Christ being wrought into humanity. The building of the Church cannot be manufactured with human hands, by imitating a pattern or by forming an organization. Of course, by the birth and growth of life a certain pattern will spontaneously come forth, just as the size and shape of a man evolve by his birth and growth in life. No one can manufacture or fashion a man to his present form. Even so, the building of the Church is not a man-made pattern, not a manufactured imitation, but the spontaneous growth of Christ as our life.

Every part and every aspect of the tabernacle typifies either the *work* or the *Person* of Christ—it is much more than a pattern. The tabernacle shows that, by means of His redemptive work, Christ Himself must be wrought into us as everything. The altar in the outer court typifies the all-inclusive death of Christ on the cross, which has accomplished a right relationship with God. Confessing that we are sinners and that we have been put to an end by His death, we receive Him as our life. Then the cleansing and purging work of His Spirit, as typified in the laver, purifies us from the dirt of the world in order to make us fit and suitable for Him to be wrought into us.

After these two items, we can then look into the building. Immediately we see that in everything it manifests Christ as having been wrought into us. Nearly everywhere in the holy place and in the Holiest of all is wood overlaid with gold, signifying that the human nature is overlaid with the divine nature, divinity has been wrought into and upon humanity. The showbread table, the lampstand, the incense altar, the ark, all the boards which form the framework of the tabernacle, and even the four layers of the covering reveal and emphasize one thing: Christ as the very embodiment of God has been wrought into us that we may experience Him as life and as everything.

The Lord must open our eyes and impress us with all these things. We cannot merely find a pattern from the book of Acts, set up elders and deacons and call this the church. This is not the church; this is an imitation of the church. If we ask someone how he came into being and became such a tall person, he will tell us, "I was born of my mother, I have eaten a lot of nourishing food, and I have grown up to such a height." We can manufacture a toy or a doll, but there is no way for us to manufacture a man. The church is a real man; no one can make a church! It must be something of new birth in the Spirit and growth of life in Christ. We must say again and again: Brothers, keep hands off! We should not try to form or organize anything.

In so many places during the last few years I have pleaded in this way, yet not many brothers realize what I mean. They say, "Well, if we do not form a church, if we do not organize anything, what should we do?" We should do one thing: eat Christ and drink of Christ. Moreover, we have to be swallowed up by Christ. The more we feast on Him, the more we will be swallowed up by Him. We think we are only feeding on Him and enjoying Him, but actually the more we feed on Him, the more we are being swallowed up by Him. The church cannot be formulated and organized, but must be born of Christ in the Spirit; it must be the living Body of Christ grown up with the life of Christ. Then, as a result, it will spontaneously assume a certain shape, and a pattern will be seen. It grows with Christ, by Christ, and in Christ.

In the outer court we experience the accomplished work of Christ, which is the means for us to enter into the holy place. The holy place and the Holiest of all are not a matter of experiencing the work of Christ but of experiencing Christ Himself. Here Christ Himself is experienced as the food for the supply of life, as the light of life, as the resurrection savor, and as the all-inclusive One. Once Christ is worked into us, the materials are available for the building of the Church. Then we will be united and built up together into one through the Holy Spirit, who regenerates and matures us (as portrayed in the golden rings and the golden bars). This is the Body of Christ; this is the dwelling place of God. Again we repeat: the building of the Church is a matter of growth, which is Christ being progressively wrought into us as everything. This alone produces the materials for the building of the Church. Through the process of regeneration and maturity by the Spirit, all these materials will be fitly framed together and united as a whole. This building in oneness is the Body of Christ and the dwelling place of God.

THE CHURCH COVERED BY CHRIST
AS THE EXPRESSION

But we must realize that even up to this stage the tabernacle is still without a roof to cover it. Regardless of the degree to which we have been wrought into Christ and Christ has been wrought into us, we are only the boards—none of us can become the covering. If we are the covering, the church will become the expression of man. Only Christ can be the covering, for the church must only be the expression of Christ Himself. In the type of the tabernacle, as we have seen, the roof consists of four layers, and every layer is an aspect of Christ. The entire roof is the revelation of Christ as the only covering. The tabernacle thus becomes an expression of Christ by this covering, which completely covers it. After the covering was put on the tabernacle, nothing but the covering could be seen from the outside. Even the boards and the utensils were inside the covering. This covering not only *protected* all the boards and utensils in the tabernacle, but also *expressed* the whole tabernacle. In fact it is the expression that protected all the boards and utensils. This means that if we do not have Christ as our expression, we do not have His protection. If we expect Christ to protect the church, we must have Him as our expression.

In some places it seems that the church is not covered by Christ, but rather by some kind of doctrine. In other places the covering is a manifestation of certain kinds of gifts—gifts have become the roof. Groups of believers are either under the covering of teachings or under the covering of gifts—not under the covering of Christ. But the gifts and the teachings can never protect us. No gifts, no teachings, no doctrines are adequate to cover a group of believers. Only Christ must be uplifted, only Christ must be exalted, only Christ must be expressed as the roof to cover us.

If we read the measurements of the tabernacle, we will discover that the covering includes not only the roof but also the two sides. From the outside nothing can be seen but the covering. The sockets, the boards, and the contents within are not visible. This means that those outside must see only Christ as the covering of the church. When people come inside the tabernacle, they see nothing but the mingling of Christ with man. Outside it is nothing but Christ, and inside it is nothing but Christ wrought into and mingled with humanity. In other words, when I am outside looking at the church, I see only Christ, but when I come into the church and look at the people, I see the mingling of Christ with every person. This is the real church. From without people can see nothing but Christ, and from within they see nothing but Christ wrought into many persons.

This is a wonderful picture. If I had more than ten Epistles like Romans, twelve like Corinthians and sixty like Ephesians, without this picture I could not be so clear. I am a simple little child, still needing pictures and drawings. When we are teaching children in kindergarten, we need some pictures. For example, to spell C-A-T to these children does not convey what is meant. We need to bring a picture of a cat and show it to them. Likewise, by beholding this picture of the tabernacle we can understand the real building of the church. It is not a matter of a pattern or an organization, nor is it any kind of formation by human hands, but it is *Christ* wrought into many persons, and they now uplift Christ and exalt Christ and put on Christ as their expression in order to cover and protect themselves.

Now let us look into the four layers of the covering. From within is the first layer of the finest materials—curtains of fine twined linen with embroidery of cherubim and beautiful colors of blue, purple, and scarlet wrought into them. Blue means heavenly, purple means royalty, and scarlet stands for redemption. The basic material, however, is the fine linen, which symbolizes the humanity of Christ with all His fine characteristics and behavior. The four Gospels give a record of a Man with both His human nature and conduct exactly like the fine linen. It is so fine, yet very strong, and because it is made of twined linen, it is doubled in strength. The Lord Jesus is so fine, yet He is so strong; there is nothing in Him that is crude or weak.

The embroidery of the cherubim means that God's glory is manifested in His creation. The cherubim typify God's glory, and the embroidered work of the cherubim on the fine linen means that God's glory has been wrought into humanity and into His creation. While Jesus was on this earth, we can realize that in this Man with His fine human nature and character God's divine glory was wrought into His creation. He is a real Man with a fine human nature and conduct, but He is also the embodiment of the glory of God wrought into His creation. He as Man is the very effulgence of God's glory. In other words, upon Him are the embroidered cherubim. Can you follow this kind of language? He is not only human, but He is also divine. His human nature bears the divine glory. We cannot exhaust this matter, but we must go on.

The second layer consists of goats' hair. In the types of the Scriptures, goats are figures of sinful men. Matthew 25:31-46 speaks of the division and difference between the sheep and the goats, and the goats are shown to be the sinful people. This corresponds exactly to 2 Corinthians 5:21: God made the One who knew no sin to be sin for us. Therefore, the layer of curtains made of goats' hair typifies Christ, who was made sin for us. Though He is the fine linen, He was made goats' hair: He has no sin and does not know sin, but He was made sin for us.

Following the layer of goats' hair is a layer of rams' skins, dyed red. The color red means the shedding of blood in Christ's redemptive work. He was the sinless One, who was made sin for us to bear our sins—this simple sentence explains the first three layers. The first layer typifies Him as the sinless One, the second that He was made sin for us, and the third layer signifies that He bore our sins and shed His blood to redeem us.

After the rams' skins dyed red, there is the fourth layer, which becomes the outer covering. This covering is formed of badgers or seals' skins, which are very strong; it can stand against any kind of weather, any kind of attack. The outer covering is not so attractive in appearance and is somewhat rough. Today, Christ is not outwardly pleasant to the worldly people: He looks just like the strong badgers' skin, unappealing in its outward appearance. Yet, though He is not so comely without, He is beautiful, wonderful, and heavenly within. He is not like today's Christianity with her huge, beautiful buildings—outwardly pretentious, but inwardly and spiritually ugly, empty, and sometimes corrupted. The worldly Christian organizations are indeed ugly. Within the proper church, the building of God, there is something heavenly and beautiful, yet without it is humble and rough, having no comeliness or beauty.

I wish to take this opportunity to say that we all must try to hide ourselves. We must never put a picture of ourselves in the newspaper. That is not something of the Church, but entirely of the fallen, worldly religion of Christianity. Oh, brothers, if possible, do not allow anyone to advertise your name in the papers. The Lord Jesus never advertised Himself. We read in the four Gospels how He always tried to hide Himself and, if possible, to keep Himself hidden. Beauty and comeliness must be the experience of Christ *within* our spirit. That is the real beauty before God.

I would take this opportunity to say a further word— about the building of meeting halls. Brothers, if possible, we should have a hall very plain and simple in appearance. Do not build a luxurious and beautiful hall. We cannot attract people *to the Lord* by beautiful external buildings. I was in Rome once and saw the so-called Peter's Cathedral. I cannot tell how many millions of dollars the building is worth or how many people are drawn there daily. When I was there it was crowded. But I am afraid that not one person out of a thousand was saved. What is the advantage of drawing people by such means? I would say, if possible, we ought to get rid of this kind of building. It is not a pleasure, but an offense to the Lord.

My emphasis, however, is not on these matters, but on the very *Christ* who is full of beauty within and so simple and humble without. Such a Christ must be the expression of our testimony and the covering of the church. This is not man's opinion or thought; this is the picture shown by the Word of God. We must not put up anything else as an expression. We must only lift up and exalt our wonderful Christ as the covering of God's building—a Christ within who is full of divine comeliness, and a Christ without who is so simple and humble in the eyes of the world. It is such a church that can endure any assault and stand against any temptation. Once the attack of the enemy comes, those in the beautiful buildings of the so-called Christian churches will be the first to fall. Only those who do not bear any outward show but have the heavenly beauty and divine comeliness within them will endure to the end. *Christ* is their content and their covering. Nothing can damage or overcome the real building of the church covered with such a Christ.

Let us learn to put these things into practice and to seek Him in the spirit. Let us learn to discern our spirit and experience Him as everything to us. Then we will have the measure of the fullness of Christ and become available material to be built up with others as the building of God covered by Christ as the expression. Then there will be a proper, strong church, which can withstand any attack, endure any trial, and overcome any temptation for the ultimate glory of God.

CHAPTER TWENTY-THREE

THE CHURCH—
GOD MANIFESTED IN THE FLESH

"But if I tarry long, that thou mayest know how men ought to behave themselves in the house of God, which is the church of the living God, the pillar and ground of the truth. And without controversy great is the mystery of godliness; He who was manifested in the flesh, Justified in the spirit, Seen of angels, Preached among the nations, Believed on in the world, Received up in glory" (1 Tim. 3:15, 16).

There are three aspects of the Church mentioned in verse 15: the "house of God," "the church of the living God," and "the pillar and ground of the truth." Verse 16 continues with the great mystery of godliness, which is God manifested in the flesh. How are these two verses related? Some rightly insist that a semi-colon at the end of verse 15 is better than a period indicating a full stop: "The pillar and ground of the truth; and without controversy, great is the mystery of godliness; He who was manifested in the flesh...."

THE CHURCH—THE HOUSE OF GOD

Why is the Church mentioned together with the manifestation of God in the flesh? It is because the Church is the house of God. What does the term "the house of God" mean? When you refer to "your house," you mean the place where you dwell, where you live, where you work out your life; and that is just the meaning of the house of God. It is not a light or loose term. "The house of God" is the place where God dwells, where He lives, and where He works out His life.

This house is none other than the Church of the living God. Notice that the term here is not merely "God," but "the living God." He is so living; and He now dwells in the Church, moves in the Church, lives in the Church, and works out His whole life in the Church. When we say that the Church is the house of God, we must have a very deep realization that God dwells, lives, and works out His life in this house. Do we have such a deep understanding concerning the house of God?

THE CHURCH—THE PILLAR AND GROUND OF THE TRUTH

This Church is not only the house of God, in which God dwells, lives, and works out His life, but it is also the pillar and ground of the truth. What is truth? Do not think that truth means doctrine. The word "truth" in such a passage means *reality*. Nothing is real in the whole universe, nothing is truth; everything is but a shadow. Everything that can be seen, everything that can be touched, everything that can be possessed and enjoyed is not real, but at best a shadow. Whatever exists in this universe is but a shadow, not the real thing.

What is the real thing? It is *Christ* as the reality of everything. The food you take is not the real food, but only a shadow of the real food. The real food is Christ. If you do not have Christ, you do not have the reality of food. You may think that the human life you have is real, but it is not; it too is only a shadow. Real life is Christ. If you have the Son of God, you have life; if you do not have the Son of God, you do not have life (1 John 5:12).

If a brother sends you a photo of himself, you will say, "This is Brother so and so." But in truth, that is not Brother so and so. It is only a picture, and a false picture at that. In fact, all pictures are false, for real things are not found in pictures. The whole universe is nothing but a picture. All the types, all the figures, all the shadows in the Old Testament were but pictures of the reality to come, which is Christ Himself. Christ is the truth, Christ is the reality of the whole universe, Christ is the reality of the Old Testament and also of the New Testament. If you just have the teaching about Christ, you do not have the reality of Christ. Christ Himself is the truth, and His Spirit is the Spirit of truth (John 14:17;

15:26; 16:13; 1 John 5:6). He Himself is the reality, and His Spirit is the Spirit of reality.

The Church, in which this living God dwells, lives, and moves, is the pillar and ground upon which the reality stands. It bears the reality. *Within* this Church the living God dwells, and *upon* this Church the truth, the reality, stands. We are not standing for doctrine, but we are standing for Christ, the reality, the truth. We should be able to say, "Friends, come and see; come to the Church and see the reality of the universe. Come and see the reality of life, the reality of love, the reality of patience, and the reality of many other things."

One afternoon in 1933 while I was visiting Brother Watchman Nee, he suddenly asked, "Brother, what is patience?" At first, I thought this was a childish question. I was taught what patience was when I was a small child. But since the question came from his mouth, I should not take it lightly; so I considered further: "What does he mean 'What is patience?'" I dared not answer. He was sitting in a rocking chair, rocking back and forth. Finally I ventured, "Patience is something by which one suffers and endures the ill treatment of others. That is patience." Then he said, "No!" I asked, "Well, Brother, if patience is not endurance, please tell me what it is?" As he continued to rock in his chair, he continued asking, "Well, what is patience? What is patience?"

After a long period, he suddenly answered, *"Patience is Christ."* It was very short and very simple. "Patience is Christ." I simply could not understand this kind of "foreign" language. I said "Brother, that sounds strange to me. I don't understand. Please tell me what you mean?" He would not say anything else but kept repeating, "Patience is Christ, patience is Christ." For the whole afternoon we did not talk about anything else. I was more than puzzled.

After three or four hours I left him, very much disappointed. Returning to my room, I knelt down and prayed: "Lord, tell me what it means 'patience is Christ'? I cannot understand." Finally the Lord showed me that our patience must be Christ Himself. Patience is Christ living within me and through me. Ah, when I saw this, it was a real revelation! I was so happy!

We must realize that human patience, which we can attain by ourselves, is not the real patience. Human patience is only a form and a shadow; the real patience is Christ. Everything that we need—patience, humility, kindness, love for others, and even love for God—must be found in Christ Himself. Even the ten commandments are just a shadow; Christ is the reality. If we have Christ living out through us, we have the reality and fulfillment of all the requirements of the ten commandments.

The Church must bear the truth, the reality. The Church must be the pillar and ground of this universal reality, which is Christ Himself. We must be able to tell others: "Come to the Church and see the real patience and the real humility. Come to us and see the real faithfulness and the reality of being honest."

In the Church God dwells, because the Church is the house of God. God lives, God moves, and God works out His life *in the Church;* and the testimony and the reality stand *upon the Church.* We must consider these two aspects: *inwardly,* God's dwelling in the Church; and *outwardly,* the Church bearing the testimony and the reality. These two aspects show the real mingling of God with man. Within the Church—this group of redeemed, regenerated, and trans- formed people—God dwells; and upon this group of people, there is the reality of the universe. All the reality of the uni- verse is centered in this group. If anyone wants to know what life is, he must come to the Church and see. If some would like to know what love is, they too must come and see. If the reality of humility and kindness is to be known, the Church is the place to see it. Upon this group of people is seen the real- ity of the all-inclusive Christ. The testimony of the Church is not in doctrine but in bearing Christ as the reality. The more we exclaim "Christ," yet have not the inner reality, the more Christ is gone. We only have Christ in shouting, in talking, and in teaching. We do not have Him in our *inner life,* nor do we experience Him in our *outer living,* our daily walk. The Church must be the pillar and ground, bearing Christ as the only reality of everything. If we do not know the real meaning of life, we must be able to come to the Church to find it.

THE CHURCH—THE MANIFESTATION
OF GOD IN THE FLESH

This is the right meaning of "the house of God" and "the pillar and ground of the truth." This Church is the *continuation* and the *multiplication* of "God manifest in the flesh." This is the reason why the Apostle Paul put these two verses together. The manifestation of God in the flesh has very much to do with the Church being the house of God and the pillar and ground of truth. When we are the living Body of Christ in a certain place, we are really the house of God and the pillar and ground of reality. We are then the *increase,* the *enlargement,* of the manifestation of God in the flesh. God manifests Himself again in the flesh, but in a *wider* way. The principle of the New Testament is the principle of the incarnation, which simply is: God Himself manifest in the flesh. In other words, God is mingled with human beings—not in an outward way, but in an inward way. The Church is the manifestation of God, not the manifestation of doctrines or gifts. The Church must have God in Christ through the Spirit manifested, not the doctrines or gifts demonstrated.

NOT BUILT BY OUTWARD CHANGE

We are burdened because we fear many brothers and sisters unconsciously think that we are going to *form* a new movement or train people to *form* a new pattern for the church. This is our real concern. We must all look to the Lord that this kind of thought and understanding may be entirely abandoned. It must be one hundred percent out of our blood. We are not here with the intention of forming a new movement. No! A hundred times no! If we do, it simply proves that we do not know God's economy. I must stress again and again that the Church is not something formed according to a certain pattern. The living God dwelling in us is not a matter of doctrine. According to their daily walk most Christians today do not know the way of inner life and Christ as their life. This really troubles us and burdens us. When people get a certain kind of realization or learn certain methods, they try to start something new where they live. This is not the Lord's way.

What we need today is not just a change of clothes but a change of blood. The natural blood must be changed. We need not only to change the outward way, but the inward life. Suppose a person was formerly a pastor with the title "Reverend." Perhaps he was even dressed in a clergyman's robe with his collar turned backwards. Then he received the light that all these things are wrong: the titles "Pastor" and "Reverend" are wrong, the collar turned backwards is wrong, and the black robe is wrong. So he got rid of all these things; he crossed out the clergyman's title and began to wear ordinary clothes. After this, he went to work for the Lord at another place and in another way, without the title and without the robe.

Whether this is right or not, I would not like to say, but I do wish to say one thing: we must find out whether a real change has taken place within such a person. No doubt he has dropped all those former things, but this change is too outward. Formerly this person was ministering by himself, by his natural life. Now he has a change in the outward things, but is there any change in his inward life? It is quite probable that he is still working and ministering for the Lord by the same life he had when he used the title. Though he had a real change outwardly, yet inwardly he is still the same. Such a change as this simply becomes an outward movement. Formerly he practiced the "church" by voting and forming an executive committee; now he drops that and gathers a group of elders. Although this is a real change, nothing is changed in the inner life. The outward change is not the result of an inward change in life, so it becomes just another new, religious movement.

Moreover, we must go beyond the change in the inner life and realize the Church. The Church is *a mingling of God with man*. The reason we have spoken so much about the soul, the spirit, and the heart is because this helps us to realize that God is our content and we are His containers. We must know how to adjust our heart so that we may open our heart and let Him come in; and we must know how to exercise our spirit in order to contact Him, contain Him, and even digest Him. For example, suppose you eat steak for dinner. When you have contained this steak in your stomach for four hours, it will be digested and become the very constituent of your body. This is the true picture of the Church. But present Christianity is more a religion than the reality of life. The problem today is not just a change of form outwardly, but a change of life inwardly.

NOT BUILT BY MERE TEACHINGS

Furthermore, we should not give attention only to the teachings. In order to help us, allow me to use a simple illustration. When I was a boy, I and many others studied in a Christian school and received Christian education. We were taught with the stories of the Bible. Although we were not saved, most of us were brought into Christianity and learned the doctrines. Many times we argued with people that Christianity was the right religion. The missionaries ministered all the doctrines and teachings to us. We learned that God is a God of three Persons—the Father, the Son, and the Spirit. We learned that Christ was born of a virgin and lived, walked, and worked on this earth; and we even believed that He was resurrected. But if you asked us, "Are you saved?" we did not know. To us God and Christ were only terms. I have to testify that by that time, hardly any of the several hundred members in that church were clear about salvation. They were known, however, as "Christians." Sometimes all the members of the church paraded on the streets, holding up crosses and singing, "Onward Christian Soldiers." I share this in order to illustrate how empty mere teachings are.

Today some insist on ministering a set of teachings such as predestination, free-will, absolute grace, and eternal security. You can minister all these teachings, but the life and the spirit within people may never be touched. To continue my testimony, one day a member of our family was saved, and then I got saved. We finally had a real touch with God, and life touched us deeply within and wrought a real change. Even the outward living and the outward walk were changed. The real change in our lives influenced others also to be saved. Thereafter we knew that we must have something more than teachings. All the teachings in Scripture must simply be a vehicle to transmit Christ into us. If they do not fulfill this purpose we are desperately short of something.

NOT BUILT BY MERE GIFTS

The same principle applies to the matter of gifts. Many Christians today think that since they have the gifts they are quite spiritual. But in fact, it is not so. If you read 1 Corinthians, you can see the state of the Corinthian believers. They exercised the gifts even more than the Apostle (1 Cor. 14:18-20), but did they have the real growth of life? No; they were carnal and childish (1 Cor. 3:1-3). As the teachings must be the means to convey Christ to others, so also the gifts must only be the means to convey Christ. God's intention today is not to give us so many teachings and gifts, but to minister and impart Christ into us.

Here is a real incident. I met a person who was full of the knowledge of the Bible; but as he talked about the Bible, he was smoking. After talking about the book of Matthew and the ten virgins for half an hour, he said, "Excuse me, I have to smoke a little. I know this is wrong, but I am weak." Then he went into the book of Revelation and talked about the ten horns, the seven heads, and the forty-two months. He had the strength to teach, but eventually he had to say, "Excuse me, I have to smoke a little more." Though he was so strong in Bible teaching, he was very weak in the spiritual life.

I also saw many people speaking in tongues. After the demonstration, they were so careless in their daily living. Some were even more careless than unbelievers. It was so easy for them to lose their temper at home. All these things simply prove one thing, that God's intention is not to give us teachings and gifts, but to give us Christ, the living One. He uses the teachings, when given in a proper way, to convey Christ to us; and sometimes He uses certain gifts as the means to minister Christ to us and stir up people to receive Christ. But we all must realize that God's intention is that we may know the living One, the Triune God, and experience Christ in the Holy Spirit.

Do you remember the story in the Old Testament of an ass which spoke a human language? That was genuine speaking in tongues! I doubt whether all the tongues are as genuine today. I read an article recently in which the writer reported that he had contacted more than one hundred persons speaking in tongues. He said every one without an exception doubted whether the tongue he spoke was genuine. Yet the writer still encouraged people not to doubt, but to continue their experience. After I read that, I said to myself, "At the time of Pentecost, did Peter doubt whether the tongue he spoke was genuine? Was there anyone at that time who had such doubts?" But today, why do so many people question whether or not their tongue is genuine? The simple answer is that so many tongues today are not genuine.

But even if you are speaking a genuine tongue, I must tell you that is not the life. Even King Saul received the outpouring of the Holy Spirit (1 Sam. 19:22-24), but do not think that he experienced life. On the contrary, it simply exposed him. After he received the outpouring, he made himself naked! This illustrates that the outpouring of the Holy Spirit is different from the life. The life is not the outpouring; the life is only Christ Himself in the Spirit.

Oh, brothers and sisters, I do beg that you will try your best to understand I am not trying to criticize, but I am really sick with my burden. When I see the desperate situation of the Lord's people, I do not know what to say, nor what to do. When the teachings are taught, people are so responsive. When the gifts are mentioned, many are stirred up. But when the inner life and the indwelling Christ are ministered, how great is the need for an inner revelation. The doctrines and the gifts are outward, but Christ is hidden within. Oh, how the Lord's people need to know this indwelling One, who is so living and powerful—converting, regulating, strengthening, refreshing, and always transforming and saturating us.

NOT BUILT BY POSITION

We must also see that the building of the Church is not a matter of position or responsibility but a matter of life in the inner being. It is not a matter of putting someone into a position, but it is the growth to maturity of the inner life. The inner being must be wrought by God through His inward working. The more we put people into position, the more we will have nothing. But the more we help people to realize the growth of life, the more the life will multiply. The growth of the inner life is the sure way of building up the Church. Then through matured life we will be spontaneously qualified to exercise responsibility.

Again, we need to repeat: God's intention is to impart Christ into us and make Christ everything within us. God uses the teachings to help some, He uses the gifts to help others; but these are not the main thing. Inner revelation is needed to see the goal of the living Christ dwelling within us. Then, wherever we are meeting together, we are the living house of the living God. The living God dwells, lives, and works in us; and we bear the testimony of Jesus, who is the reality of this whole universe. Then we will have a real manifestation of the living God in the flesh. This is the way of God's recovery today. Let us look to the Lord for the inner grace that we may have the reality of the Church.

CHAPTER TWENTY-FOUR

THE VISION
OF THE MARK OF GOD'S ECONOMY

The economy of God with its mark was given at the beginning of this book, but after reading all these chapters, it is still possible to miss it. In simple words, God's economy is to work Himself into us, and in order to accomplish this He must do it in three Persons—the Father, the Son, and the Spirit. From the beginning of this book we have spent much time in this economy of the Triune God. God never intended to give us the doctrine of the Trinity in the Scriptures. The doctrine only involves us in many different concepts. But the Scriptures do reveal how God accomplished His divine economy in three different Persons.

We have pointed out that the word "economy" in the Greek means administration, stewardship, government, arrangement, dispensation. The word dispensation is used without any thought of periods of time, but with the meaning of the dispensing of God into us. Again, we repeat, God's intention is to dispense Himself into us. This plan is the center of His creation and redemption. God created and redeemed man for this purpose, that man might be the container into which He could dispense Himself. In the whole universe—time, space, and eternity—the center of God's economy is to dispense Himself into humanity.

Eventually, the ultimate consummation of all God's work of creation, redemption, and transformation is the universal mingling of God with man. Thus, the New Jerusalem comes into existence as the ultimate result of all God's work as recorded in the sixty-six books of the Scriptures. This result is nothing other than the universal mingling of God with man. The New Jerusalem is a mingling of God Himself with a corporate body of people. At that time they will no longer be natural, but every part and every aspect will have been regenerated, transformed, and conformed by God and with God as life. They will have been transformed in nature and conformed in appearance to God Himself. If we are going to serve the Lord in a proper way, we need to have this vision. This vision is not new; it is the original vision from the beginning of the Church age. But it must be new and renewed day by day in us. It must be the controlling vision of all our work, life, and activity.

THE MARK ACCOMPLISHED THROUGH FOUR STEPS

What is the mark of this economy? First of all, the Father, who is the source, has been put in the Son. The Father with all His fullness has come forth in the Person of the Son. The Son is both the embodiment and the expression of the Father; no one but the Son has ever seen God the Father. In the Son God has accomplished all that He planned by four major steps: incarnation, crucifixion, resurrection, and ascension. These four steps have fulfilled all that God planned in eternity.

By incarnation, God was brought into man. God has been brought into the human nature and has lived in it for thirty-three and one-half years on this earth. Whatever human sufferings there were on this earth, God has suffered. It was not just a man by the name of Jesus who suffered, but it was God within Him who was suffering.

Next was the crucifixion. All the twelve negative items such as Satan, the fallen man, sin, the world, death, etc., have been brought to the cross and put to an end. All the negative things were terminated at the cross.

The resurrection followed the crucifixion. The resurrection recovered and uplifted the standard of humanity created by God and brought the human nature into God. By incarnation the divine nature was brought into man; by resurrection the human nature was brought into God. Now it is possible for man to have more than a created human nature, for his nature has been regenerated, uplifted, and brought into God.

After the resurrection, Christ was exhibited to the whole universe as a "model." In this model God is in man and man is in God. Since all the negative things have been dealt with and terminated by the cross, there is nothing negative in this model.

This model then ascended to the heavens and was enthroned with glory and authority. The human mind cannot apprehend this picture. At this point everything was accomplished; nothing was left unfinished. This model, which is God mingled with man and man mingled with God, ascended far above all things in space and in time. He transcended to the highest place in the universe and was enthroned with glory and authority.

Then from this glorified One the Holy Spirit came like the outflow of a liquid composed of many elements. The divine nature, the human nature, the human life, the human suffering, the death of the cross, the resurrection, the ascension, and the enthronement are all elements included in the Holy Spirit. As we have seen, this wonderful outflow is the "all-inclusive dose"—whatever we need is in this "dose." As this outflow the Holy Spirit has been poured into us. On the day of resurrection and on the day of Pentecost, the Holy Spirit of Jesus, the Spirit including all the elements, came *into* and *upon* the early Christians. On the one hand, He comes *into* us, and on the other hand, He comes *upon* us. God in His three Persons mingles Himself with us.

THE MARK OPERATING IN THE HUMAN SPIRIT

The mark of God's economy is this: God in three Persons has come *into* us. The New Testament deals more with the fact that God in the Spirit has come *into* us than with the fact of His coming *upon* us. This little word "in" occurs many times in the New Testament—Christ "in me," Christ "lives in me," Christ "formed in me," Christ "makes His home in me," "abide in me and I in you," etc. If you have time, count how many times this little word has been used in the New Testament. God made man purposely in three parts so that He could come into man and man would fit His purpose. Man, as we have seen, is a tripartite being—body, soul, and spirit—corresponding to the Tabernacle

with its three parts—the outer court, the holy place, and the
Holiest of all. Only the inmost part is the place where God's
Shekinah glory dwells and where the ark as the type of Christ
stays. This shows us clearly that God and Christ have come to
dwell in our spirit. Our spirit is the inmost part as the Holiest of
all.

We can trace this from the Scriptures very clearly, especially in 2 Timothy 4:22: "The Lord be with thy spirit." Also,
in Ephesians 4:6, God the Father is in us; 2 Corinthians 13:5,
God the Son is in us; and Romans 8:11, God the Spirit is in us.
The Triune God in the Persons of the Father, the Son, and the
Spirit is now in our spirit. Here is the mark of God's economy:
the Triune God is in our spirit to be our life and everything.
Oh, how God's economy has been neglected in the past centuries by His children! We must recover this mark of God in our
spirit.

Using our spirit as His center, God works Himself out
through us. The Triune God is in the center of our being. This
is most wonderful! God came into the human nature, brought
the human nature into the divine nature, and put an end to
all negative things; now the Triune God and all that He has
accomplished are in our spirit as our life and everything.
From this central point the Triune God spreads out to saturate the inward parts of our being with Himself. The human
spirit is the very spot of the mark of God's economy. If we miss
this spot, we simply miss the mark of God's economy. I do not
say this is the *goal* of God's economy, but the *mark*. This mark
has been neglected by most Christians today. We may talk
about many Scriptural things and not hit this spot! In fact,
we must realize that all the teachings of the sixty-six books of
the Bible are for this mark. All the different gifts and all the
different functions are for this mark and must be centered
upon this mark.

How can we realize the Triune God indwelling our spirit?
How can we experience this indwelling Spirit in our spirit? We
must realize that the Triune God is always *working* within us
(Phil. 2:13). He is working within us, not without us; and He is
even working within us more than upon us. The Greek word
"working" is equivalent to the English word "energizing." The

indwelling God is energizing within us all the time. He is also *living* within us through Christ who "lives in me." In other words, the Triune God is within us today as our life. With this life there is also the inner law, the living law—not the law of letters, but the law of life. This divine law of life is always *regulating* us from within (Heb. 8:10). Besides inwardly regulating us the indwelling Triune God is also *anointing* within us all the time (1 John 2:27).

Let us consider these four words further—working, living, regulating, and anointing. How much the Church needs the inner revelation and experiences of these four things! We should not consider them as teaching, but we should experience the Triune God everyday working in us, living in us, regulating us, and anointing us. We should allow this wonderful Triune God to continually regulate us in our thinking, in our motives, in our words, in our attitudes, and in our relationships with others. Even our eating and our clothing should be regulated by Him. We must experience Him to such an extent and in such a practical way. This must not be degraded into a doctrine; doctrine does not work. When this is practiced, it will be revolutionizing. We must realize that such a wonderful Christ is indwelling our spirit for the purpose of working and living in us, and regulating and anointing us.

THE MARK BUILDING UP THE CHURCH

If we do not experience Him in such a practical way, it is absolutely impossible to build up the Church. This is illustrated in the type of Eve, who was brought into being by coming out of Adam (Gen. 2:21-24; Eph. 5:30-32). Eve was a part of Adam, something out of Adam. Only that which came *out of* Adam could be the wife to Adam. Every part and every aspect of Eve was something of Adam. This confirms that the Church can only be built with that which is out of Christ. Doctrines and gifts do not build the Church. Christ Himself in the saints is the only material with which the Body of Christ is built. If we lack the experiences of practically living by Christ, we will only be a certain kind of "religious church."

Furthermore, we must learn to experience Christ not only as our life, but also as our food, the Bread of Life. He is the food supply within us. Day by day we have to feed on Christ and be nourished by Him. This must not be merely a teaching to us, but our daily and hourly experience. In John 6:57 the Lord says that he that eats Him shall live by Him. If we are going to live by Christ, we must eat Him; then He will be so real to us. It is sorrowful that many Christians are not eating Christ daily.

Let me illustrate in this way. When you were born you probably weighed between six to eight pounds, but now you are over 100 pounds. Your body has been built up; but please tell me, by what? By going to the restaurant and looking at menus? Of course not. Your body was built up by the things you ate, by so many eggs, chickens, potatoes apples, bananas, and so forth. How, then, can the Body of Christ be built up? Not by teaching, for the more you are taught how to eat, the more you will be reduced. In fact, if you only *learn* the art of eating, we will soon have a funeral for you. You may learn many things and even be the best dietitian, but you will soon die! Even so, you may know all the good, scriptural, and even spiritual teachings, and yet be starving from the lack of food. The churches today need the "mothers" to nurse the young ones and give them not teachings, but something of Christ to eat and drink.

If you ask me what is troubling me these days, I will tell you only two things: One is that although so many dear brothers and sisters have really seen the negative things of Christianity and something about the Lord's way with His church, I am afraid they will practice the church life by outward methods. You say, "Formerly I pastored a church in a certain way, but now I see that is wrong. So I will drop that way and use another way." This is still a religious activity, *not* the building up of the Body of Christ. The building up of the Body of Christ is something from *within*. You must feed on Christ, eat Christ and drink Christ so that you will be nourished with Christ. When you are full of Christ, you will minister something of Him as food to others. Then the Body of Christ will be built up.

It is not a matter of method. If you read the whole New Testament, you cannot discover one method. If I have any method at all it is this: first, you must be put on the cross;

second, you must feed on Christ in the spirit day by day; third, when you are nourished and full of Christ, you need to nourish others with *Christ*. Then the church will come into being. The only method is to go to the cross, feed on Christ, and nourish others with Christ.

The other thing that troubles me is this: Though we have been talking so much about Christ as our life, I fear that we only know this as a message, as a term, as a subject; we do not have the daily and hourly experiences. We need to be continually regulated and anointed by Him. Daily and hourly we must feed on Him and have intimate fellowship with Him. We need to forget about ourselves and contact Him, enjoy Him, be regulated by Him, and anointed by Him all the time. This is the inner life, the inward experience of the indwelling Christ. I would recommend to you the book written by Andrew Murray, entitled, *The Spirit of Christ*. It will be a great help—not to gain knowledge, but to experience the indwelling Christ in your daily life. As you let Christ be your daily food, you can testify to the whole universe: "I am tasting Christ day by day. I am having such an intimate, living fellowship with Him hour by hour. I am under His regulating and His anointing all the time." We all need to pay full attention to this matter. This is the mark of God's economy. If we miss this mark of God's economy in our spirit, how can His economy be worked out in the Church? When you drive your car, you know where to put the gasoline and where to start it; that is the mark of running your car. If you lose that mark, though you may have a very beautiful car, it will not run!

This is why the book of Hebrews gives us such a verse as chapter four, verse twelve. The Word of God is so living and penetrating that it divides our spirit from the soul. All the experiences taught in the book of Hebrews must be realized by discerning the spirit. The all-inclusive Christ as the good land is in the spirit, and His dwelling in the Holiest of all is also in our spirit. If you do not know how to discern the spirit from the soul, you will miss the mark and cannot enjoy Christ. Everyday, you must deal with the living Christ, who is so subjective to you. Christ is within you, and He is so living, so real, and so practical. When you eat Him, drink Him, and feast on Him as your daily nourishment, you will live by Him and with Him and be under His constant regulating and anointing. This is what we need to experience all the time if we are going to impart Christ as food to others. If people are fed with Christ, He will become the material in them, and then the Body of Christ will gradually grow and be built up. I do look to the Lord that our eyes will be opened to see the heavenly vision and the inner revelation of this living, indwelling, subjective Christ in our spirit as the mark of God's economy.

ABOUT THE AUTHOR

Witness Lee was born in 1905 in northern China and raised in a Christian family. At age 19 he was fully captured for Christ and immediately consecrated himself to preach the gospel for the rest of his life. Early in his service, he met Watchman Nee, a renowned preacher, teacher, and writer. Witness Lee labored together with Watchman Nee under his direction. In 1934 Watchman Nee entrusted Witness Lee with the responsibility for his publication operation, called the Shanghai Gospel Bookroom.

Prior to the Communist takeover in 1949, Witness Lee was sent by Watchman Nee and his other co-workers to Taiwan to ensure that the things delivered to them by the Lord would not be lost. Watchman Nee instructed Witness Lee to continue the former's publishing operation abroad as the Taiwan Gospel Bookroom, which has been publicly recognized as the publisher of Watchman Nee's works outside China. Witness Lee's work in Taiwan manifested the Lord's abundant blessing. From a mere 350 believers, newly fled from the mainland, the churches in Taiwan grew to 20,000 in five years.

In 1962 Witness Lee felt led of the Lord to come to the United States, settling in California. During his 35 years of service in the U.S., he ministered in weekly meetings and weekend conferences, delivering several thousand spoken messages. Much of his speaking has since been published as over 400 titles. Many of these have been translated into over fourteen languages. He gave his last public conference in February 1997 at the age of 91.

He leaves behind a prolific presentation of the truth in the Bible. His major work, *Life-study of the Bible,* comprises over 25,000 pages of commentary on every book of the Bible from the perspective of the believers' enjoyment and experience of God's divine life in Christ through the Holy Spirit. Witness Lee was the chief editor of a new translation of the New Testament into Chinese called the Recovery Version and directed the translation of the same into English. The Recovery Version also appears in a number of other languages. He provided an extensive body of footnotes, outlines, and spiritual cross references. A radio broadcast of his messages can be heard on Christian radio stations in the United States. In 1965 Witness Lee founded Living Stream Ministry, a non-profit corporation, located in Anaheim, California, which officially presents his and Watchman Nee's ministry.

Witness Lee's ministry emphasizes the experience of Christ as life and the practical oneness of the believers as the Body of Christ. Stressing the importance of attending to both these matters, he led the churches under his care to grow in Christian life and function. He was unbending in his conviction that God's goal is not narrow sectarianism but the Body of Christ. In time, believers began to meet simply as the church in their localities in response to this conviction. In recent years a number of new churches have been raised up in Russia and in many eastern European countries.

OTHER BOOKS PUBLISHED BY
Living Stream Ministry

Titles by Witness Lee:

Abraham—Called by God	0-7363-0359-6
The Experience of Life	0-87083-417-7
The Knowledge of Life	0-87083-419-3
The Tree of Life	0-87083-300-6
The Economy of God	0-87083-415-0
The Divine Economy	0-87083-268-9
God's New Testament Economy	0-87083-199-2
The World Situation and God's Move	0-87083-092-9
Christ vs. Religion	0-87083-010-4
The All-inclusive Christ	0-87083-020-1
Gospel Outlines	0-87083-039-2
Character	0-87083-322-7
The Secret of Experiencing Christ	0-87083-227-1
The Life and Way for the Practice of the Church Life	0-87083-785-0
The Basic Revelation in the Holy Scriptures	0-87083-105-4
The Crucial Revelation of Life in the Scriptures	0-87083-372-3
The Spirit with Our Spirit	0-87083-798-2
Christ as the Reality	0-87083-047-3
The Central Line of the Divine Revelation	0-87083-960-8
The Full Knowledge of the Word of God	0-87083-289-1
Watchman Nee—A Seer of the Divine Revelation ...	0-87083-625-0

Titles by Watchman Nee:

How to Study the Bible	0-7363-0407-X
God's Overcomers	0-7363-0433-9
The New Covenant	0-7363-0088-0
The Spiritual Man 3 volumes	0-7363-0269-7
Authority and Submission	0-7363-0185-2
The Overcoming Life	1-57593-817-0
The Glorious Church	0-87083-745-1
The Prayer Ministry of the Church	0-87083-860-1
The Breaking of the Outer Man and the Release ...	1-57593-955-X
The Mystery of Christ	1-57593-954-1
The God of Abraham, Isaac, and Jacob	0-87083-932-2
The Song of Songs	0-87083-872-5
The Gospel of God 2 volumes	1-57593-953-3
The Normal Christian Church Life	0-87083-027-9
The Character of the Lord's Worker	1-57593-322-5
The Normal Christian Faith	0-87083-748-6
Watchman Nee's Testimony	0-87083-051-1

Available at
Christian bookstores, or contact Living Stream Ministry
2431 W. La Palma Ave. • Anaheim, CA 92801
1-800-549-5164 • www.livingstream.com